Beginning Syntax

D0954964

To my very unique Dad, with love

Beginning Syntax

Linda Thomas

BLACKWELL
Oxford UK & Cambridge USA

Copyright © Linda Thomas, 1993

The right of Linda Thomas to be identified as author of this work has been
asserted in accordance with the Copyright, Designs and Patents Act 1988.

First published 1993

Reprinted 1993, 1994, 1995, 1996, 1997 (twice), 1998, 1999

Blackwell Publishers Ltd
108 Cowley Road
Oxford OX4 1JF, UK

Blackwell Publishers Inc.
350 Main Street
Malden, Massachusetts 02148, USA

All rights reserved. Except for the quotation of short passages for the purposes
of criticism and review, no part of this publication may be reproduced, stored
in a retrieval system, or transmitted, in any form or by any means, electronic,
mechanical, photocopying, recording or otherwise, without the prior permission
of the publisher.

Except in the United States of America, this book is sold subject to the condition
that it shall not, by way of trade or otherwise, be lent, re-sold, hired out, or
otherwise circulated without the publisher's prior consent in any form of binding
or cover other than that in which it is published and without a similar condition
including this condition being imposed on the subsequent purchaser.

British Library Cataloguing in Publication Data
A CIP catalogue record for this book is available from the British Library

Library of Congress Cataloging in Publication Data
Thomas, Linda.
Beginning syntax/Linda Thomas.
p.   cm.
ISBN 0–631–18827–4 (alk. paper) — ISBN 0–631–18826–6 (pbk: alk. paper)
1. Grammar, Comparative and general – Syntax. I. Title.
P291.T49   1993   92–39658
415–dc20   CIP

Typeset in 10 on 12pt Sabon
by TecSet Ltd, Wallington, Surrey
Printed and bound in Great Britain by T. J. International Ltd,Padstow, Cornwall

This book is printed on acid-free paper

Contents

Preface and Acknowledgements

Studying language can take varied forms, but sooner or later students come to a point when they need a systematic understanding of basic grammatical concepts and terminology. As a student you may, for example, be studying language variation or change, or child language acquisition, or analysing literary language, or as a trainee teacher you might be interested in grammar in terms of the National Curriculum. To be able to draw comparisons or make meaningful generalizations, you will need a framework in which to work. The purpose of this book is to provide you with such a framework.

I have used earlier versions of the book in undergraduate courses where students required a background analytic knowledge. In many cases the students I have taught have had no experience of formal grammar teaching and needed to start from scratch. So in this book I have assumed no prior knowledge of grammatical analysis of any kind. The text uses simple material and offers, in the form of practical exercises, a chance to get to grips with each new idea before moving on to the next one. In this way, I hope that the myth that grammar is 'hard' will be dispelled. I have summarized the material covered in each chapter at the end for easy reference in the form of 'rules to remember'. You should bear in mind though, that no 'rule' is ever infallible, and as you progress through the text you may find yourself beginning to challenge some (or all) of the assumptions made and explanations given in the text. If this happens, do not worry: it's a healthy sign.

Some of you may never need to progress beyond what is offered here in that your requirements are for a basic understanding of syntax which you can apply to other data. Others may be intending to study linguistic theory at an advanced level and need a suitable starting point. Once you have

viii   *Preface and Acknowledgements*

become confident in handling the basic terms and concepts presented here, you may find it easier to contend with a level of analysis that calls for an understanding and evaluation of different syntactic theories.

The level and pace of this book are pitched to provide you with an introductory text that enables you to walk before you run. I hope it will satisfy your needs, whatever they may be.

My thanks are due to Karen Atkinson, Deborah Cameron and Jennifer Coates who used earlier drafts of this book with their students and made recommendations for amendments and additions based on the feedback they received. I am grateful to them, their students and mine for their comments and suggestions. I am also indebted to them, to Janet Goodwyn and to Shan Wareing for the encouragement and support they have given throughout the time I have been working towards the final text.

My grateful thanks also go to my family, Patrick, James and Elizabeth, for their patience.

Abbreviations

A	adjective
A	adverbial
Adv	adverb
AdvP	adverb phrase
AP	adjective phrase
AUX	auxiliary
complex	complex-transitive verb
coord	coordinator
deg	degree adverb
DET	determiner
ditrans	ditransitive verb
dO	direct object
intens	intensive verb
intrans	intransitive verb
iO	indirect object
MOD	modal
N	noun
NP	noun phrase
oC	object complement
P	preposition
P	predicator
part	particle
PASS	passive
PERF	perfect
pO	prepositional object
POSS	possessive

PP	prepositional phrase
prep	prepositional verb
pres	present tense
PRO	pronoun
PROG	progressive
S	sentence/clause
S	subject
*s*C	subject complement
trans	transitive verb
V	verb
Vgp	verb group
VP	verb phrase

1 Tools for Analysis

Introduction

Languages are by nature extremely complex and describing a language, any language, is not an easy task. To help with description and analysis it is considered easier to divide a language into separate components or different areas of analysis. Such areas include for example PHONOLOGY, which looks at and describes the sound system of a language, MORPHOLOGY, which looks at the way words are formed, SYNTAX, which seeks to describe the way words fit together to form sentences or utterances, and SEMANTICS and PRAGMATICS which study meaning. Although these components overlap and interact with each other, they can to some extent be looked at and described individually.

We are here primarily concerned with syntax, or sentence structure. This means looking at the way words combine together in a language (in this case English) to form sentences. One way to study syntax is to look at sentences which we already know to be considered syntactically 'well-formed' sentences to the speakers of that language. For example:

(1)   I shot the sheriff

would be considered by native speakers of English to be a syntactically well-formed sentence, whereas:

(2)   the shot sheriff I

would not. This idea of a sentence being syntactically well formed will become clearer as we progress. By analysing or describing sentences such as

(1) in terms of their constituent parts, we can see the patterns that words follow when they fit together.

Perhaps the best way to make this clear is to practise it by looking at some examples of English sentences. The examples used will be based on written rather than spoken language. This is because written language tends to be more explicit and complete. There is no other speaker present to interrupt you, or finish your utterance for you, or throw you off your point. Neither can you leave a statement unfinished because you assume that the other person 'knows what you mean'. Also the example sentences we use will consist of sentences in isolation rather than as part of connected discourse. Again this is because sentences in isolation have to be totally explicit to convey meaning. For instance, 'I have' may be perfectly acceptable as part of connected discourse, say in response to the accusation 'you haven't done the dishes', but it wouldn't be very meaningful on its own. Using written language and sentences in isolation, then, we can hope to grasp the main concepts before using the analysis on spoken language.

So how do we set about describing a sentence in English? Well, it seems clear that sentences are made up of units and that at one level these units are words. So: **a sentence consists of words** or alternatively **words are CONSTITUENTS of a sentence.**

We can write this in a different way with a convenient shorthand. Using **S** to stand for *sentence*, and an arrow, →, to mean *consists of*, we can say that:

(3)   S   →   word + word + word + word + word + . . .
      (sentence) (consists of)

You can use this to describe any sentence. Try it with:

(4)   Beanz meanz Heinz
(5)   I don't know what Jennifer will do when she finds out that she didn't turn the gas off before she went to work this morning

Using the formula at (3), you should end up with the following analyses:

(6)   S   →   word + word + word
        (sentence (4))   (consists of)   (Beanz + meanz + Heinz)

(7)   S   →   word + word + word + word + word +
        (sentence (5))   word + word + word + word + word +
                                        word + word + word + word + word +

word + word + word + word + word +
word + word + word + word + word

This analysis is reasonable as far as it goes but it suggests that, apart from the number of words, sentences (4) and (5) are the same. The situation isn't really that straightforward. First, the sentence at (5) appears to be much more complicated than the one at (4) and not just because of the number of words it contains. The analysis we have used doesn't capture that complexity. Second, the formula we have used for analysis has two purposes. It not only serves to describe an already existent sentence (like the ones at (4) and (5)), but also to tell us that this is the way in which we can make countless other sentences in English. In other words, it says that to make a syntactically well-formed English sentence all you have to do is string together a series of words. To see if this works, I suggest you make up two or three sentences using words from the following list:

(8)   girl, that, the, likes, apple, buys, this, eats, dog

and following the formula:

(9)   S → word + word + word + word + word

If we were to randomly select words as the formula suggests, we could presumably have:

(10)   *Girl apple likes this that

This string of words, I think you'll agree, does not make up a well-formed English sentence; the words are all English words, but they do not appear in an order you would normally expect. Certain sorts of words, it seems, can only appear in certain positions or in certain combinations. Word order is very important in English (although this doesn't mean that it carries the same importance in all languages). When a sentence is produced that is not syntactically well formed it is said to be UNGRAMMATICAL and is preceded like (10) above by an asterisk.

Word Categories

Clearly there are rules governing the way in which words can be put together to form syntactically well-formed or GRAMMATICAL sentences:

the study of syntax aims to discover them and to describe and analyse language in terms of these rules. To begin to do so, let's look at a grammatical sentence, for example:

(11)   The girl likes the dog

This appears to be reasonable (if a little unexciting). What about:

(12)   The dog likes the girl

Here we have changed the word order but the sentence still works. This suggests that the words *dog* and *girl* are interchangeable. In other words, in a sentence like this, either word will do in either position. Of course changing the words over changes the meaning but the sentence is still well formed; it is still a grammatical sentence. There are, however, words on the list which cannot be used in the same position as *dog* and *girl*. For example:

(13)   *The girl likes the **this**
(14)   *The **buys** likes the apple

In other words it seems that because *girl* and *dog* are interchangeable they are the same type of word. They belong to the same WORD CATEGORY. There is one other word on the list which can be used in the same position as *girl* and *dog*; that is *apple*, as in:

(15a)   The **girl** likes the **apple**
(15b)   The **apple** likes the **girl**
(15c)   The **dog** likes the **apple**
(15d)   The **apple** likes the **dog**

Here we run into a bit of difficulty and you may wonder why the sentences at (15b) and (15d) do not have an asterisk since they don't seem to make much sense. The reason is that the problem with these sentences lies with the meaning, or the ideas being conveyed, and not with the grammatical structure. The study of meaning in a language falls into the sphere of semantics, which put simply looks at the relationship of words and their meanings to each other, and **pragmatics**, which looks at the relationship of words to the real world. Now, it is not normal in the real world for apples to be capable of liking anything, so the sentences appear odd. However, if you were to imagine a fantasy world, such as in a child's story book, where apples can happily become animate and engage in all sorts of activities otherwise reserved for humans or animals, then it becomes perfectly possible for apples to like girls, dogs or anything else they choose. In writing such a story you would need the facility to produce sentences such as those at (15b) and (15d), which are grammatical sentences. It is important to keep in mind the distinction between an ungrammatical sentence and one with an 'odd' meaning.

Nouns Substantiv/navnefom

To return to the example sentences, we can see that the words *girl*, *dog* and *apple* can all be used in the same positions to produce a grammatical sentence (although the meaning changes each time). That means they all belong to the same word category. This category is called NOUN.

  Nouns are often described as being the 'name of something' including people and places and we'll stick with this definition for the time being, although there are some difficulties with it. For instance, it may be fairly simple to sort out words like *table* or *chair* which refer to concrete things, things we can see or touch, but abstract concepts like *love* or *sincerity*, or names of days of the week, such as *Monday*, are not quite so easy to determine as 'things'. Nevertheless the words which represent these ideas are nouns. The 'name of something' definition is to some extent a semantic one. That is, it suggests that we have to rely on knowing the meaning of the word in order to be able to categorize it. This isn't necessarily true; we can and do use other clues as we shall see later.

  However, on the above definition, we can now extract the nouns from the list of words given at (8):

  NOUNS: girl, dog, apple

Using the term *noun* and the shorthand outlined at (3) above we can describe all the sentences at (11), (12), and (15) as follows:

(16) S → the + NOUN + likes + the + NOUN
          girl   girl
          dog   dog
          apple   apple

In this way we can use one formula to describe several sentences. What the formula at (16) does is to tell us that in a sentence with this order or structure we can put any noun on the list in the appropriate place and the sentence will be grammatical. There might be some strange meanings but the sentences will still be grammatical.

Determiners   fastScætter

If we return to example (11) (*the girl likes the dog*) you can doubtless pick
out two other words which are not nouns but are of the same type as each
other; i.e., *the*. You can now pick out the other words on the original list
which could be put in place of *the*; that is, *this, that*.

(17a)   **This** girl likes the dog
(17b)   **This** girl likes **that** dog
(17c)   **This** girl likes **this** dog
(17d)   The girl likes **that** dog
(17e)   The girl likes **this** dog
(17f)   **That** girl likes the dog
(17g)   **That** girl likes **that** dog
(17h)   **That** girl likes **this** dog

These sentences can of course be repeated with *dog* in the place of *girl* and
girl in the place of *dog*, and so on.

Again, *this, that* and *the* are interchangeable. They also therefore belong
to the same word category, DETERMINER. Determiners are a small group
of words and they act to limit or determine to some extent the possible
range of things which the noun can refer to. For example, the noun *girl* can
refer to any girl in the entire universe; if we add *this* as in *this girl* in sentence
(17a), we are limiting the meaning to one specific girl.

The basic determiners are the ARTICLES:

INDEFINITE ARTICLE: *a, an*
DEFINITE ARTICLE: *the*

Advertising slogans can usefully illustrate the distinction between the
indefinite and the definite article. For example:

utydelig

(18)   Twix: **the** longer lasting snack

not

(19)   Twix: **a** longer lasting snack

Assuming that advertisers want to create as favourable an image of their
product as possible, and then want to convey that image as precisely as
possible, they must choose their words very carefully. '*The* longer lasting
snack' is clearly a unique product, not one among many.

A word is a determiner if it can be used in place of, but not with an article:

(20a) **The** longer lasting snack
(20b) **This** longer lasting snack
(20c) ***The this** longer lasting snack

passende for 20b

There are other determiners which we will come back to in due course (pp. 83–5). We can now extract the determiners from the original list of words.

DETERMINERS: *the, this, that*

Perhaps you can begin to see why it's useful when describing sentences to be able to put words into categories. Instead of having to write out every example of how individual words can be put together to form a sentence as in the examples at (17), then write them all out again substituting different nouns, we can say these sentences consist of:

erstatte/ indsætte

(21) S → DETERMINER + NOUN + likes + DETERMINER + NOUN
e.g. this	girl	that	dog
that	dog	the	apple
the	apple	this	girl etc.

In other words we can describe the structure of this sentence without saying what each word actually is but rather what type or category of word can be used. Where a determiner is indicated any determiner can be used; where a noun is indicated any noun which normally functions with a determiner can be used. *angivet*

Verbs *Udsagnsord/ Verbum*

We are now left with *likes* from the example sentence. Given the sentence:

(22) This girl **likes** the apple

pick out the other words on the original list (8) we could replace *likes* with.

They are:

(23a) This girl **eats** the apple
(23b) This girl **buys** the apple

Likes, eats, buys are all VERBS. As the examples below show, we can only replace a word with another of the same type or category. In this case, with another verb:

(24a)   This girl **eats** the apple
(24b)   *This girl **dog** the apple
(24c)   *This girl **that** the apple etc.

So what exactly is a verb? One definition which is sometimes given is that a verb is a word which describes an action, as in:

(25)   The girl **buys** the apple

or a state, as in:

(26)   The girl **is** happy

This isn't an entirely satisfactory definition but will do for now.
    If we go back to the list of words at (8) we can now extract the verbs.

    VERBS: likes, eats, buys

So we can now say that a sentence in English can consist of:

(27)   S → DETERMINER + NOUN + VERB + DETERMINER + NOUN

e.g.	the	dog	likes	the	apple
	this	girl	buys	that	dog
	that	dog	eats	the	apple etc.

and that in the determiner space we can put any one of a number of determiners, in the noun space we can put any one of a number of nouns and in the verb space we can put any one of a number of verbs. Look at your original example sentences. Do they all fit the pattern at (27)?
    This isn't the only way of making a sentence in English but it is one way and if you think of all the determiners, nouns and verbs there are in the English language, there is a fair number of sentences you could make up just using this format. Using general categories means we can describe all these sentences in just five words.
    Describing a sentence in this way (example (27)) is an abstraction. We are dealing with the structure of the sentence at an abstract level. Normally no one goes around saying (or writing) 'Determiner noun verb determiner noun.' But individual speakers produce particular sentences which conform

to this abstract pattern. So it's conceivable that an English speaker might produce one of the following in some context or another:

	DETERMINER	NOUN	VERB	DETERMINER	NOUN
(28a)	This	dog	chased	that	girl
(28b)	The	hen	ate	the	corn
(28c)	That	woman	drives	a	tank

and so on.

These examples all contain different words and have different meanings but they share the same STRUCTURE or FORM. That is, all the example sentences can be described in the **same** way.

Tree Diagrams

Another way of representing this abstract structure is in diagramatic form. Because the diagram has branches it is called a TREE (although like a family tree it is upside down). Using a tree diagram the formula at (27) becomes:

(29)

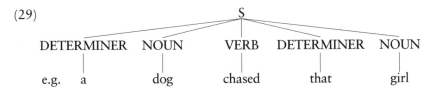

DETERMINER	NOUN	VERB	DETERMINER	NOUN
e.g. a	dog	chased	that	girl

As stated before, both types of formula serve two purposes. First, they describe sentences that we already know are grammatical sentences of English; and second, they serve as a pattern or template to make more sentences with. In other words, if we follow the pattern these formulae represent we should, by and large, come up with some reasonable English sentences. This gives us a much more detailed and informative description than the one we originally used at (3), which only states that a sentence consists of words. This new description tells us something about both word order and the kinds of words which can go together. It describes sentences in terms of the **categories** the individual words belong to. So as well as saying that individual and specific words (e.g. *girl, boy, this, that, likes, sees* etc.) are **constituents** of a sentence, we can also say that **word categories** are **constituents** of a sentence.

ood terbindelse / oodgeuppe

Phrases and Phrase Structure

However, to stop at the level of word categories misses out some important facts. One is that in sentence (29), for instance, we have the same pattern of constituents before and after the verb (that is DETERMINER + NOUN). These two words also appear to belong together more closely than say the noun *dog* and the verb *chased* and if in fact we turn the sentence around to get:

(30)   **That girl** was chased by **a dog**

you can see that it is not only the nouns which change places but that they take their determiners with them as well. Another way of illustrating that these words belong together is to give the 'girl' and the 'dog' a name. Names of specific items such as individual people, animals, places (for example streets, towns, countries), days of the week, months of the year and so on are called PROPER NOUNS. All other nouns are COMMON NOUNS. Both types of noun can appear in the noun space. If we imagine that the girl in example (29) is called *Carol* and the dog is called *Henry* we get:

(31)   **Henry** chased **Carol**

By substituting a proper noun for a common noun we have had to replace both the determiner and the noun, not just the noun.

You can get the same result by using a PRONOUN. The pronoun for female beings is *she/her*, for male *he/him* and for neuter *it*. (There are others which we will return to later (pp. 80–3).) The term 'pronoun' suggests that this is an item which can be used in place of, or on behalf of (pro) a noun. But it is not that simple. Taking the example at (29) and substituting pronouns for the nouns we get:

(32)   *A **he/it** chased that **her**

There is a choice of pronoun for *dog* since it is normal to refer to animals by either *he, she* or *it*. It is not usual to refer to humans as *it*, unless to make a specific point about the sub-human characteristics of an individual, as a sister might in talking about her brother. The example at (32) however is not a well-formed sentence.

Go through the following example sentences and substitute pronouns for nouns.

(33a)   A dog chased that girl
(33b)   The girl likes the dog
(33c)   The girl eats the apple
(33d)   The dog wants a bone
(33e)   That hen ate the corn
(33f)   The detective found a clue

tilegner Sig

Whichever pronoun you have considered appropriate, you will see that only by substituting a pronoun for the determiner **and** the noun can you produce a grammatical sentence. For example:

(34a)   The dog wants a bone
(34b)   *The he wants a it
(34c)   He wants it

(35a)   The detective found a clue
(35b)   *The she found a it
(35c)   She found it

This suggests that in these examples and the example at (29) the pair of words DETERMINER + NOUN, functions as a single unit. The pronoun replaces the entire unit. We can therefore re-write the formula at (27) as follows:

(36)   S → (DETERMINER + NOUN + VERB + (DETERMINER + NOUN))

What we're now saying is that there is a unit or constituent which can consist of two words, DETERMINER + NOUN (e.g. *that girl*), or one word, NOUN (e.g. *Carol*), PRONOUN (e.g. *she*). Whether it consists of one or more than one word this unit is called a PHRASE. A phrase, then, can be a unit or constituent within a sentence (S) which itself contains other units or constituents. So we can change the diagram at (29) to:

(37)

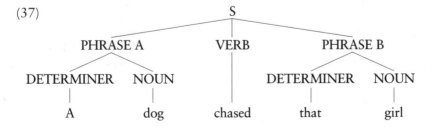

and the description at (36) to:

(38)   S → PHRASE A + VERB + PHRASE B

This description will also cover examples like (31). That is, the sentence *Henry chased Carol* consists of a PHRASE A *Henry*, a VERB *chased* and a PHRASE B *Carol*. The tree diagram will look like this:

(39)

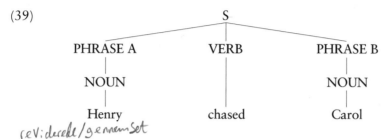

reV: derell/gennamSet

A revised example (32), *He/It chased her* consists of a PHRASE A *he/it*, a VERB *chased* and a PHRASE B *her*. Using **PRO** as the shortened form of PRONOUN, the tree diagram will look like this:

(40)

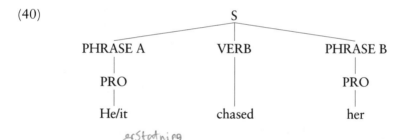

erStatning

This method of substituting one form for another (e.g. PROPER NOUN/ PRONOUN for DETERMINER + NOUN) is a good way of finding out whether or not two or more words constitute a phrase, and we will be using it again later on.   *udgøre*

    A pronoun then replaces not just a noun, but an entire phrase, in this case a NOUN PHRASE. Just as words can belong to different categories, so too can phrases. We have already said that PHRASE A and PHRASE B in example (37) are the same in that they both consist of a determiner followed by a noun. Probably the most important part of this combination is the noun. Certainly it is the noun which gives us most information. If you can imagine a typical newspaper headline based on the example at (37) it might read:

(41)   Dog chased girl

It is most unlikely to read:

(42)   A chased that

This kind of phrase is therefore called a NOUN PHRASE or **NP** for short. (We will look at noun phrases in much more detail later.) Using the shortened form **DET** for DETERMINER, the descriptions at (37) and (38) can now be written:

(43)

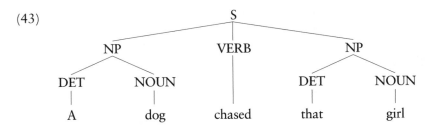

and

(44)   S → NP + VERB + NP

Exercise 1

Draw tree diagrams for the following sentences. Check your answers on page 129.

Example: The dog wants a bone

1. Carol likes Henry
2. The hen ate the corn
3. She loved it
4. Joe kicked James
5. He hates him
6. The detective found a clue

Form and Function

Subject

We now have a framework for description that tells us that certain kinds of words can be grouped together in certain patterns to form sentences. Presumably there is a reason for this patterning. Why in all our examples is there a noun phrase at the beginning of the sentence, before the verb? If there is no purpose or if it serves no function then why not put it somewhere else? Take the example sentences at (33) and try moving constituents around so that the NP doesn't come first.

Moving the noun phrase in the example at (33a) for instance results in:

(45a)   *Chased that girl **a dog**
(45b)   *Chased **a dog** that girl
(45c)   That girl chased **a dog**

The first two examples are not grammatical in English. The third is, but the meaning has changed. (You might have noted that we have also returned to the NP + VERB + NP structure that we started with.) One way in which the meaning has changed is that the dog is no longer doing the chasing; that activity has transferred to the girl. Neither is the girl on the receiving end of the chasing any more; that dubious honour has transferred to the dog. But changing the noun phrases around has also changed the focus of our attention. That is, we're no longer talking about the dog, but about the girl, first introducing her and then saying something about her (i.e. that she chased a dog). The girl has become the SUBJECT (*S* for short) of the sentence. In (33a) the dog is the subject, being introduced first, then having something said about it (i.e. that it chased the girl). Changing these noun phrases around has changed our understanding of the way the constituents relate to one another. Go back through all the examples used so far (ignore those at 18), (19) and (20)) and you should be able to pick out the subjects. All the subjects occupy that first NP slot. In example (33a) then, the constituent *a dog* can be described as both a **noun phrase** and the **subject** of the sentence. This difference in definition is the difference between FORM and FUNCTION; a **noun phrase** is what the constituent is, **subject** is what it acts as or does. So although both *the dog* and *the girl* are noun phrases, their functions differ according to their position in the sentence. (We will look at the function of the noun phrase following the verb shortly (pp. 17–18).)

Predicate kort karakteristik

The rest of the sentence is called the PREDICATE. We've already noted that what follows the subject is what is said about it and that is precisely what the term **predicate** means. We can now divide all our sentences into this two-way division, subject and predicate. For example:

opdeling

(46a) This girl likes that dog
       SUBJECT = this girl; PREDICATE = likes that dog
(46b) The dog wants a bone
       SUBJECT = the dog; PREDICATE = wants a bone

By considering sentences in terms of the functions of subject and predicate we can divide them initially into just two constituent parts. We have already determined that the <u>subject of a sentence takes the form of noun phrase</u> (NP), but what form does the predicate take? In these examples the predicate consists of a verb and a noun phrase but that may not always be the case. The <u>predicate can consist of a verb on its own</u>, for example:

(47a) The dog **barked**
       SUBJECT = the dog; PREDICATE = barked
(47b) Carol **cried**
       SUBJECT = Carol; PREDICATE = cried

or it can be more complex (predicates are in bold type):

(48a) The boy **laughed**
(48b) The cow **jumped over the moon**
(48c) Tom **sang for his supper**
(48d) Carol **gave the dog a bone**
(48e) He **died peacefully**
(48f) The cat **sat on the mat**

In all cases, however, the predicate contains a verb and where it consists of only one word, that word is a verb. The form of the predicate is that of VERB PHRASE (**VP**). <u>A verb phrase can contain one constituent</u> (e.g. VERB, as in *Carol **cried***) or more than one constituent (e.g. VERB + NP, as in *The dog **wants a bone***). (There are other types of constituent shown in the examples at (48) which we will be considering in more detail later on (pp. 37–55).

    To show that the verb phrase constitutes one complete unit of a sentence we can use a similar test to the one we used to show that a noun phrase constitutes a complete unit. With a noun phrase we substituted a pronoun for a noun phrase; with a verb phrase we can substitute *does/did too*. For example:

(49a)   This girl **likes that dog**
        This boy **does too**

(49b)   Carol **cried**
        Sally **did too**

(49c)   The dog **wants a bone**
        The cat **does too**

(49d)   The boy **laughed**
        The girl **did too**

til fælde

In each instance we understand *does/did too* to replace an entire verb phrase. In other words, in their full forms these sentences would read:

(50a)   This girl **likes that dog**
        This boy **likes that dog** (too)

(50b)   Carol **cried**
        Sally **cried** (too)

(50c)   The dog **wants a bone**
        The cat **wants a bone** (too)

(50d)   The boy **laughed**
        The girl **laughed** (too)

You can try this test with the other examples at (48). In the same way that we said the pronoun replaces an entire noun phrase (e.g. DET + NP) so the form *does/did (too)* replaces an entire section of the sentence, the predicate or verb phrase.

On a tree diagram the two-way split into noun phrase (subject) and verb phrase (predicate) looks like this:

(51a)

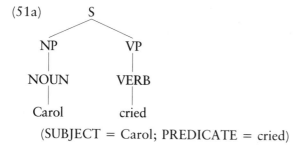

(SUBJECT = Carol; PREDICATE = cried)

(51b)

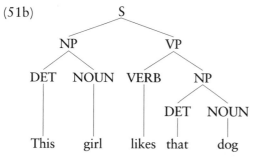

(SUBJECT = this girl; PREDICATE = likes that dog)

What we're saying here is that in the first analysis a sentence (S) can consist of (→) a noun phrase (NP) and a verb phrase (VP), or:

(52)   S → NP + VP

The verb phrase at (51b) looks more complicated than the one at (51a) because of the noun phrase contained within it. The verb phrase at (51b) can be represented as:

(53)   VP → VERB + NP

Apart from functioning together as the predicate these two constituents (verb and noun phrase) each have a further function. Because it is indispensible in the predicate, the term <u>PREDICATOR (**P** for short) will be used for the function of the verb.</u>

This leaves the second noun phrase. In this case the noun phrase *that dog* is functioning as the DIRECT OBJECT (*dO*) of the verb *likes*. In other words, the **subject** of the sentence (what is being talked about) is *the girl* and the information we are given about her is that she likes something. The **object** of her liking in this case is *the dog*. It could equally as easily be anything from a cabbage to an astronaut. Not all verbs require an object;

those that do such as *likes* are called TRANSITIVE VERBS. We will be considering objects in much greater detail later when we look at verb phrases (pp. 37–55).

For (51a) we now have the functions:

(54)   Carol   cried
       SUBJECT (*S*)   PREDICATOR (*P*)

and for (51b):

(55)   This girl   likes   that dog
       SUBJECT (*S*)   PREDICATOR (*P*)   DIRECT OBJECT (*dO*)

More on Trees

So far we have been using two ways of representing the structure of the example sentences. One way is by the tree diagram as in the examples at (51). One advantage of this method is that the HIERARCHY of the constituents can be seen at a glance. What is meant by hierarchy is that some constituents (e.g. S, NP, VP) contain other, smaller constituents (imagine a set of Russian dolls). The larger constituents are higher up the tree or further up in the hierarchy. It is easy to see from a tree diagram just what is embedded or contained in what. Each point on the tree is called a NODE and the nodes that are higher up the tree are said to DOMINATE those that are further down. In other words, the S node dominates every other node because it is the highest in the tree. Obviously it is closer to some nodes than to others, especially the two resulting from the first division or BRANCH of the tree, namely the NP and VP nodes. It is therefore said to IMMEDI-ATELY DOMINATE these two nodes. In the same way in example (51b), the VP node not only **dominates** the VERB, NP, DET, and NOUN nodes because it is higher up the tree, but it **immediately dominates** the VERB and NP nodes because they are the first ones resulting from the **branch** at that point.

The tree diagram also gives visual information on the function of the constituents. In English, the **subject** of a sentence is that **NP** which is **immediately dominated by S** (in example (51b) *this girl*), and the **object** is that **NP** which is **immediately dominated by VP** (in example (51b) *that dog*).

Another way we have been using to represent structure is by 're-write rules', for example:

(56)   S → NP + VP

where the symbols are used to show what the sentence can consist of. In other words, whatever is on the left of the arrow can be replaced by or described (re-written) in terms of whatever is on the right. Using the shorthand versions V for VERB and N for NOUN, if we are told that:

(57a)   S → NP + VP

that:

(57b)   VP → V + NP

and that:

(57c)   NP → DET + N

we would be able to construct a sentence like that at (51b) or many of the other examples we have used so far. For example, given (57a) we get:

(58a)

```
              S
          /       \
        NP         VP
```

given (57b) we can add:

(58b)

```
              S
          /       \
        NP         VP
                  /   \
                 V     NP
```

and given (57c) we get:

(58c)

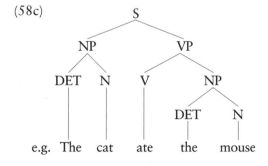

```
                    S
              /           \
           NP              VP
          /  \           /    \
        DET   N         V       NP
         |    |         |      /   \
         |    |         |    DET    N
         |    |         |     |     |
  e.g.  The  cat       ate   the  mouse
```

One of the advantages of symbolizing structure in this way is the ability to show that some constituents are optional. For instance, there are some cases where a determiner is not required to complete a noun phrase, as in example (39), *Henry chased Carol*. Plural nouns provide another example. Although they can appear with determiners, there are constructions where they don't. For example:

(59a)   Pigs fly
(59b)   Dogs hate cats
(59c)   The cats chased the mice
(59d)   That cat likes mice

To show that a determiner can be but is not always required to make a grammatical sentence, brackets are used, as:

(60)   NP → (DET) + N

We have, though, the option of using a pronoun (PRO) in the NP slot so we can also have:

(61)   NP → PRO

To indicate that there is a choice between (DET) + N or PRO, curly brackets are used:

(62)   NP → $\{$(DET) + N$\atop$PRO$\}$

The re-write rules are now:

(63)   S   → NP + VP
       VP → V + NP
       NP → $\{$(DET) + N$\atop$PRO$\}$

From these rules, then, we can make not only a sentence like (58c) using both determiner and noun in each instance, but sentences like those at (39) or (40). We can also create variations. For example we can get:

(64)   A dog chased Carol

by using the option to have a determiner in the first NP but not the second, and so on.

So why do we need these abstractions? Well, one of the main advantages as stated before is that it becomes possible to describe the structure of many sentences of English all at once. Obviously so far we have only described very simple sentences; many sentences are far more complex, so we are not saying that all sentences **have** to follow the pattern outlined or abstracted above, just that some can and do.

Symbolizing structure in this way also shows up the regularities in the way the various categories behave. For example, all nouns behave in similar ways in that they occupy certain sentence positions. They also often occur with determiners (no other category does this). Observing regularities in behaviour is one way of categorizing words or phrases. In other words we can say that a word is a noun because it behaves in the same way as other nouns. This is a better definition than the one we used earlier because it covers for example ABSTRACT NOUNS like *love*, or *sincerity* which didn't obviously fit the previous definition. The same argument applies to categorizing words as verbs and we will be looking more closely at the behaviour of verbs in due course.

Exercise 2

A useful exercise would be to try constructing three or four sentences using the rules at (57) (see example at (58), page 19). Suggested examples are given on pages 130 and 131.

Now draw tree diagrams for the following:

Example: Juliet loves Romeo

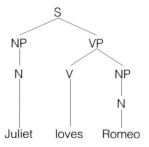

1. Alice followed the rabbit
2. He loves carrots
3. The lamb followed Mary
4. Beavers build dams
5. The cat killed the mouse
6. Jack killed the giant
7. She solved the mystery
8. The witnesses helped her
9. Students enjoy this exercise

(Tree diagrams are given on pages 130–4.)

2 More on Categories

So far we have looked at the structure of simple sentences, at the phrasal categories NP and VP, and at the word categories NOUN, DETERMINER and VERB. Needless to say, life isn't quite this simple and there are other categories which we need to describe. In this section we'll be looking at ADVERBS and ADVERB PHRASES, PREPOSITIONS and PREPOSITIONAL PHRASES, and ADJECTIVES and ADJECTIVE PHRASES.

Adverbs and Adverb Phrases

An ADVERB (or **Adv** for short) is another word category. As far as meaning is concerned, adverbs often add information in relation to circumstances of manner, time, or place; in other words, they answer the questions 'How?', 'When?', 'Where?' For example:

(1a) Ken snores **loudly**
(1b) The baby cried **continually**
(1c) He advertises **nationally**

These types of adverbs are called CIRCUMSTANCE ADVERBS. Not all circumstance adverbs end in -*ly* but very many, as in these examples, do. This helps to make them fairly easy to spot. In these examples the adverb is said to MODIFY the verb; in other words it works to more narrowly define the sense of the verb by telling something of the way it is done. For example we find out that when Ken snores, he doesn't snore softly, and so on.

In terms of a phrase category, an ADVERB PHRASE or **AdvP** can be formed by one or more constituents. (You remember we said earlier (p. 11) that a noun phrase could consist of one word, or more than one word; the same applies to adverb phrases.) For example, in:

(1a)   Ken snores **loudly**

loudly is the adverb phrase. In:

(2)   Ken snores **very loudly**

very loudly is the adverb phrase. In this case, *loudly* is the circumstance adverb (Adv) and *very* is a DEGREE ADVERB (**deg**). A degree adverb, as its name suggests, tells us to what degree something is done, as in **very loudly**. Other degree adverbs include words like *quite, too, highly, extremely, more, less, rather* and so on. Again, just as an adverb is said to **modify** a verb, so a degree adverb is here said to **modify** or limit the sense of an adverb. For instance, if Ken is snoring **very** loudly, then he can't be snoring **rather** loudly. A test to classify a degree adverb is that it cannot normally appear on its own in the AdvP slot, unlike the adverbs in the examples at (1). We would not judge the following to be grammatical:

(3)   *Ken snores **very**

An adverb phrase, then, consists of an adverb preceded optionally by a degree adverb. If you remember, the way to indicate whether a constituent is optional is with brackets, so we can show the constitution of an adverb phrase as:

(4)   AdvP → (deg) + Adv

What is the constitution of the following adverb phrases? (See page 134.)

extremely fast
seriously
too loudly

The tree diagram for (2), where the adverb phrase modifies the verb, would show the AdvP as:

(5)

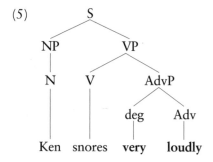

You will notice that the verb phrase (predicate) in this example consists of V + AdvP (i.e. V + AdvP are both dominated by VP). You can tell that these two constituents form the predicate by using the substitution test we used earlier (see pages 15 and 16). That is:

(6)   Ken **snores very loudly**
       Janet **does too**

where we understand *does too* to replace *snores very loudly* as an entire unit.

(7)   Ken **snores very loudly**
       Janet **snores very loudly** (too)

The structure of the verb phrase in example (5) (VP → V + AdvP) is different from the VP → V + NP structure of the earlier examples. The constituents of a VP vary according to the type of verb being used. We will look at these different verb types in due course (p. 37).

   Adverb phrases are, however, very versatile. They not only modify verbs, but adjectives and whole sentences too. We will be looking at adjectives and their modifiers later on, so for now will restrict our attention to those that modify sentences, SENTENCE ADVERBS. Sentence adverbs can appear in a range of sentence positions and often express an attitude or evaluation. They include words like *frankly, certainly, actually, perhaps, unfortunately*. For example:

(8a)   **Unfortunately** the cat killed the mouse
(8b)   The cat **unfortunately** killed the mouse
(8c)   The cat killed the mouse **unfortunately**

Tree diagrams would look like the following:

(9a)

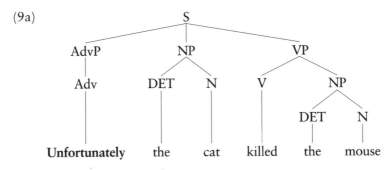

(9b)

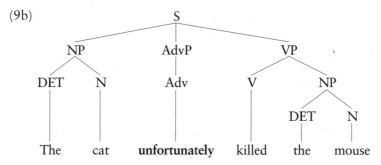

(9c)

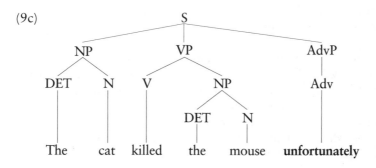

Kavck

Compare (9a), (9b) and (9c) with the example at (5). Which node immediately dominates the AdvP in (9a), (9b) and (9c), and which in (5)? How do you explain this difference?

As you will have noticed, because sentence adverbs modify the whole sentence and can appear in more than one position, the AdvP node is immediately dominated by the S node, not by the VP node as at example (5) where the adverb phrase modifies the verb. As a very general test, if the adverb phrase fits easily into other sentence positions then it is modifying the whole sentence rather than just the verb. You can check this by using a sentence adverb in the example at (5):

(10a)   **Unfortunately** Ken snores
(10b)   Ken **unfortunately** snores
(10c)   Ken snores **unfortunately**

where it fits unproblematically into a wider range of positions than *loudly*:

(11a)   ?Loudly Ken snores
(11b)   ?Ken loudly snores
(11c)   Ken snores loudly

(The use of *?* is to question grammaticality.) A sentence adverb is often differentiated in writing by a comma and in speech by a particular intonation pattern. For example:

(12)   He understands everything clearly

meaning that his understanding is clear is opposed to:

(13a)   Clearly, he understands everything
(13b)   He understands everything, clearly

meaning that it is clear to everyone else that he understands.

    Adverbs and adverb phrases are a complex feature of English and their versatility makes their behaviour hard to tie down. Tests are consequently not foolproof but can be used as a guide at this stage.

    Whether the AdvP is dominated by VP or by S, its function is that of ADVERBIAL (shorthand version *A*). If you remember, we said in chapter 1 (pp. 14–18) that the individual constituents serve a function in terms of the sentence they appear in. So in the examples at (9), the first noun phrase functions as Subject (*S*) of the sentence, the verb as Predicator (*P*), the second noun phrase as Direct Object (*dO*), and the adverb phrase as Adverbial (*A*). These distinctions (NP as *S*, V as *P*, NP as *dO*, AdvP as *A*) are, we said, the distinctions between **form** and **function**, or what a constituent **is** and what it **does**. The examples at (5) and (9) can be analysed in terms of function as:

(5)   Ken   snores   **very loudly**
        S   *P*   *A*

(9a)   **Unfortunately** the cat killed the mouse
           A   *S*   *P*   *dO*

(9b)   The cat **unfortunately** killed the mouse
         S   *A*   *P*   *dO*

(9c)   The cat killed the mouse **unfortunately**
        S   *P*   *dO*   ***A***

Rules to remember: Adverb Phrase (AdvP)

AdvP → (deg) + Adv

function: *A*

e.g. Ken snores (**very**) **loudly**

Exercise 3

Draw tree diagrams for the following sentences and analyse them in terms of function. (Check your analyses on pages 134–5.)

Example: He advertises nationally

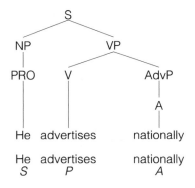

He advertises   nationally
S   *P*   *A*

1. Ken snores atrociously
2. Unfortunately, Ken snores
3. The baby cried extremely loudly
4. Frankly, she hates babies

Prepositions and Prepositional Phrases

PREPOSITIONS (**P**) belong to a small group or class of words which express relations of place, direction, time or possession. Words belonging to this class include, *of, at, to, from, till, with, for, beside, against, up, down, by* and so on. Prepositions can appear alone as in:

(14)   Sally looked **up**

or in conjunction with a noun phrase as in:

(15)   Sally looked **up the chimney**

In either case the preposition is part of a PREPOSITIONAL PHRASE (**PP**). (Remember a phrase consists of one or more than one constituent.) The prepositional phrase (PP) at (14) consists solely of a preposition (P). The prepositional phrase (PP) at (15) consists of a preposition (P) followed by a noun phrase (NP). The noun phrase in turn consists of a determiner (DET) and a noun (N). Tree diagrams are:

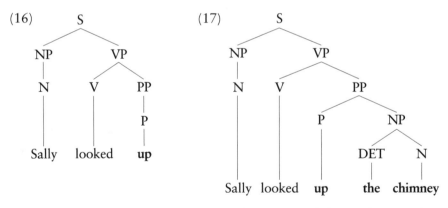

Once again you can check that the PP forms part of the predicate and is therefore dominated by the VP node by using the substitution test we used before:

(18a)   Sally **looked up**
        George **did too**
(18b)   Sally **looked up the chimney**
        George **did too**

where we understand *did too* to replace *looked up* and *looked up the chimney* respectively. That is, we understand (18a) and (18b) to mean:

(19a)   Sally **looked up**
        George **looked up** (too)
(19b)   Sally **looked up the chimney**
        George **looked up the chimney** (too)

The rule for a prepositional phrase then is:

(20)   PP → P (+ NP)

That is, in some cases a prepositional phrase will have one constituent (e.g. *up*), in some cases it will have two (e.g. *up + the chimney*). Some prepositions can only occur with a following noun phrase (e.g. *during*) in which case the option (+ NP) must be taken up.

There is a similarity in the examples at (16) and (17) between a prepositional phrase and an adverb phrase. If you remember, we said that one of the features of adverbs and adverb phrases is that they can answer the questions 'How?', 'When?', 'Where?' Here the prepositional phrase is doing the same thing by telling us **where** Sally looked. In another example, the PP might answer the question 'When?' as in:

(21)   Sally reads **in the mornings**

For this reason, the prepositional phrase is also said to function as **adverbial**. The analysis for examples (16), (17) and (21) in terms of function then is:

(22)   Sally   looked   **up**
        S   P   A
(23)   Sally   looked   **up the chimney**
        S   P   A
(24)   Sally   reads   **in the mornings**
        S   P   A

Prepositional phrases do have other functions in other contexts. We will be looking in more detail at both prepositional phrases and their functions later.

> **Rules to remember: Prepositional Phrase (PP)**
>
> PP → P (+ NP)
>
> function: *A*
>
> e.g. Sally looked **up**
> Sally looked **up the chimney**

Exercise 4

Draw tree diagrams for the following examples and analyse them in terms of function. (Check your analyses on pages 135–7.)

Example: Sally reads in the mornings

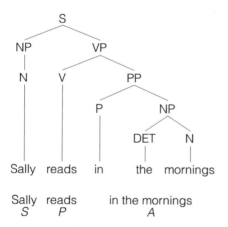

Sally reads   in the mornings
  S   *P*   *A*

1. The cow jumped over the moon
2. The boy laughed uproariously
3. The cat sat on the mat
4. The baby sleeps in the afternoon
5. The baby sleeps quite soundly

Adjectives and Adjective Phrases

ADJECTIVES (**A**) are sometimes called 'describing words' in that, as far as meaning is concerned, they define attributes or characteristics. They com-

Seed Venligvis finders/forekommer

monly occur with nouns. For instance, *the dog* and *the girl* in our earlier examples could have the adjectives *fat* and *thin* added to them:

(25)   The **fat** dog chased the **thin** girl

In this example the adjectives are said to **modify** the nouns. Just as an adverb with a verb, an adjective works to more narrowly define the sense of the noun by ascribing certain attributes or characteristics to it. For example, if the dog is fat then it can't be thin, and so on.

Again, an adjective is a constituent of a sentence both at word level and at phrase level where it becomes an ADJECTIVE PHRASE (**AP**). An adjective phrase, like all other phrases, can consist of one or more than one word. For example:

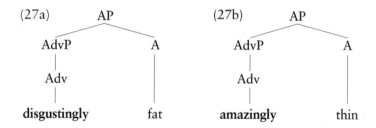

(26)   The **disgustingly fat** dog chased the **amazingly thin** girl

In (26) the adjectives *fat* and *thin* are being modified by the adverb phrases *disgustingly* and *amazingly*. These adverb phrases form part of the adjective phrase:

(27a) AP   (27b) AP

AdvP	A		AdvP	A
Adv			Adv	
disgustingly	fat		**amazingly**	thin

The adverb phrase itself can also have more than one constituent. For example:

(28)   The **quite disgustingly** fat dog chased the amazingly thin girl

where the adverb *disgustingly* is modified by a degree adverb (deg).

(29)

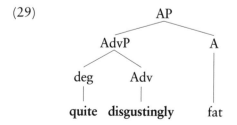

indbetatnice

The inclusion of an adverb phrase is optional so the constitution of an adjective phrase is:

(30)   AP → (AdvP) + A

When adjectives and adjective phrases work in this way to modify nouns, they form **part of the noun phrase**. You can check that this is so by substituting the pronoun *it* as we did before (see pages 10–12).

(31)
$$\left\{ \begin{array}{l} \textbf{The dog} \\ \textbf{The fat dog} \\ \textbf{The disgustingly fat dog} \\ \textbf{It} \end{array} \right\}$$
chased the girl

It is, of course, possible to modify a noun with more than one adjective as in:

(32)   The **ferocious fat brown** dog chased the girl

The analysis of noun phrases containing more than one adjective can be quite complex, so we will look at these and at tree-diagram analysis when we consider the noun phrase in more detail (see pages 85–9).

Adjectives and adjective phrases don't have to appear with nouns (although they often do). They can also appear in structures like:

(33)   The dog is **quite disgustingly fat**.

The tree diagram for this adjective phrase is the same as that at (29), but as you can see, the adjective phrase no longer appears as part of a noun phrase, as it does at (31); there is no noun for it to modify.

Many but not all adjective phrases can appear in either structure. For example we can have:

(34a)   The apple looks **juicy**
(34b)   The **juicy** apple . . .

or:

(35a)   This girl seems **unhappy**
(35b)   This **unhappy** girl . . .

but not:

(36a)   The dog is **afraid**
(36b)   *The **afraid** dog . . .

Try the following adjectives in either position:

   polar, red, asleep, hard, ill, rotten, rustic

We will discuss the function of adjective phrases later when we look in more detail at the verb phrase (pp. 46–8 and pp. 52–3) and the noun phrase (pp. 85–9).

Rules to remember: Adjective Phrase (AP)

AP → (AdvP) + A

e.g. the (**quite disgustingly**) **fat** dog
       the dog is (**quite disgustingly**) **fat**

You will no doubt be delighted to learn that these are all the categories we shall be concerned with for the time being. It is interesting that intuitively native speakers of a language know (albeit subconsciously) how these abstractions or categories work anyway. If you take a look at Lewis Carroll's famous poem 'Jabberwocky' (opposite) you'll see what I mean. Try to work out how you can follow this poem without knowing the meaning of the nonsense words and what clues you use to categorize them.

Jabberwocky

'Twas brillig, and the slithy toves
   Did gyre and gimble in the wabe:
All mimsy were the borogoves,
   And the mome raths outgrabe.

"Beware the Jabberwock, my son!
   The jaws that bite, the claws that catch!
Beware the Jubjub bird, and shun
   The frumious Bandersnatch!"

He took his vorpal sword in hand:
   Long time the manxome foe he sought –
So rested he by the Tumtum tree,
   And stood awhile in thought.

And, as in uffish thought he stood,
   The Jabberwock, with eyes of flame,
Came whiffling through the tulgey wood,
   And burbled as it came!

One, two! One, two! And through and through
   The vorpal blade went snicker-snack!
He left it dead, and with its head
   He went galumphing back.

"And hast thou slain the Jabberwock?
   Come to my arms, my beamish boy!
O frabjous day! Callooh! Callay!"
   He chortled in his joy.

'Twas brillig, and the slithy toves
   Did gyre and gimble in the wabe:
All mimsy were the borogoves,
   And the mome raths outgrabe.

Summary of Rules

Rules to remember: Adjective Phrase (AP)

AP → (AdvP) + A

e.g. the (**quite disgustingly**) **fat** dog
      the dog is (**quite disgustingly**) **fat**

Rules to remember: Adverb Phrase (AdvP)

AdvP → (deg) + Adv

function: *A*

e.g. Ken snores (**very**) **loudly**

Rules to remember: Prepositional Phrase (PP)

PP → P (+ NP)

function: *A*

e.g. Sally looked **up**
      Sally looked **up the chimney**

---

3 The Verb Phrase

In chapter 1 we saw that a **VP** (**verb phrase**) can consist of a **V** (**verb**) + an **NP** (**noun phrase**). However, the VP doesn't have to be constituted in this way. How it will look will depend on the type or CLASS of verb used. We will be looking at six classes of verb; TRANSITIVE, INTRANSITIVE, DITRANSITIVE, INTENSIVE, COMPLEX-TRANSITIVE, PREPOSITIONAL. Each of these classes of verb appears with its own obligatory constituents without which it would be incomplete. We will also be looking at a change of grammatical MOOD in the form of the IMPERATIVE.

Transitive Verb

If we look again at an example used earlier, *This girl likes that dog* (see pages 17 and 18), you will remember that we said that the NP *that dog* was functioning as the **direct object** of the verb *likes* and that the verb *likes* was a TRANSITIVE VERB. A verb phrase using a **transitive verb** normally has to have a **direct object** to be complete, as can be seen from the ungrammaticality of:

(1)   *This girl **likes**

There are many transitive verbs, for example:

(2a)   Kate **hugged** the baby
(2b)   The dog **found** a bone
(2c)   Jenny **hit** him

none of which can be used in a verb phrase without an object NP, as the following examples show:

(3a)   *Kate **hugged**
(3b)   *The dog **found**
(3c)   *Jenny **hit**

The tree diagram for (2a), now including the **verb class,** is as shown in (4a) below:

(4a)

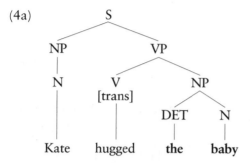

The functions of the various constituents are the same as outlined before (pages 17–18), that is:

(4b)   Kate   hugged   **the baby**
      S   P   *dO*

where, you will remember, S is short for **subject,** P for **predicator,** and *dO* for **direct object.**

Rules to remember: Transitive Verb

VP → transitive verb + *dO*
dO → NP

e.g. Kate – **hugged** – **the baby**

Exercise 5

Draw trees for the following examples, then analyse them in terms of function. (Check your analyses on pages 137–8.)

1. The dog found a bone
2. Jenny hit him
3. She broke the rules
4. The milkman sells bread

Intransitive Verb

By contrast, the INTRANSITIVE VERB, as its name suggests, is a class of verb which does not take an object. In fact an intransitive verb requires nothing else to complete the verb phrase. For example:

(5a) Ken **snores**
(5b) The baby **cried**
(5c) She **moved**

The tree diagram for this class of verb is as follows:

(6a)

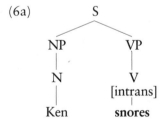

and the function of the constituents:

(6b) Ken   snores
       S   P

Rules to remember: Intransitive Verb

VP → intransitive verb

e.g. Ken – **snores**

Exercise 6

Again, draw trees for the following examples, then analyse them in terms of function. (Check your analyses on pages 138–9.)

1. The baby cried
2. She smiled
3. The dog barked
4. Jack fell

However, what has been said so far doesn't mean that **nothing** else can appear in a sentence with an intransitive verb. There are other constituents which can occur with this class of verb. However, such constituents are **optional** rather than **obligatory**. In other words, they **can** appear, but unlike the NP in a verb phrase using a transitive verb, they don't **have to**. Constituents which act as adverbials (e.g. AdvP and PP) behave in this way. So the examples at (5) can become for instance:

(7a)   Ken   snores **very loudly**
      S   *P*   *A*
(7b)   The baby   cried   **in the night**
      S   *P*   *A*

Compare the constituents labelled *A* in (7a) and (7b). There is a difference in **form** here, but not **function**. In other words, the **adverbial** (*A*) in (7a) has the **form** of an **adverb phrase** (**AdvP**), the **adverbial** (*A*) in (7b) has the **form** of a **prepositional phrase** (**PP**). Again, this a difference in terms of what the constituent **is** (its form) and what it **does** (its function).

The tree diagrams for these examples are:

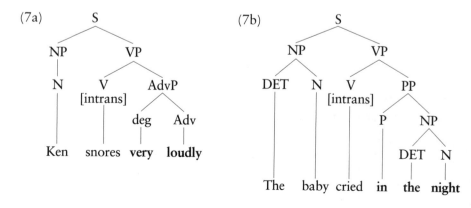

Exercise 7

Using the following examples, draw trees which show the class of the verb, then analyse the sentences in terms of function. (Check your analyses on pages 140–3.)

1. The baby slept
2. The baby slept soundly
3. The baby slept in the pram
4. Alan played the piano
5. The children played in the garden
6. The sun shone
7. She knows a secret
8. The dog snarled quite menacingly
9. Sally sang a solo
10. Sally sings in a club

Ditransitive Verb

Another class of verb which occurs with an object is DITRANSITIVE. However, this type of verb, again as its name implies, requires two objects ('di' meaning 'two'). One of these is the familiar **direct object,** the other an INDIRECT OBJECT or *iO* for short. For example, in the sentence:

(8)   Ray **told** the children a story

the verb is followed by two noun phrases, *the children* and *a story*. In a sentence with this structure it is the second noun phrase, *a story*, which is the **direct object** of the verb *told*; in other words *a story* is what is being told. The other noun phrase, *the children*, is the **indirect object** (*iO*); in other words *the children* are the recipients of the direct object, *a story*.

The tree diagram for this type of structure is:

(9a)

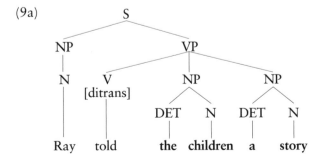

and the function of the constituents:

(9b)   Ray   told   **the children**   **a story**
　　　　S　　P　　　　iO　　　　　　dO

The verb *give* is also a ditransitive verb. In the sentence:

(10)   Sue **gave** Oxfam a jumper

you can again see that *gave* is followed by two noun phrases, *Oxfam* and *a jumper*. Again, the second noun phrase, *a jumper* is the **direct object** of the verb since that is what is being given, and the first noun phrase *Oxfam* is the **indirect object,** the recipient of the direct object.

As with a transitive verb, a verb phrase using a ditransitive verb is not really complete without both objects; they are obligatory, not optional. This is not quite as easy to exemplify because within the context of a conversation, the question *What did Sue give to Oxfam?* might receive the reply:

(11)   She gave a jumper

Such a reply would not be regarded as incomplete within that context but this is because the phrase *to Oxfam* is understood from the preceding utterance. It is not therefore necessary to repeat it (as in *She gave a jumper to Oxfam*). Without this information the reply at (11) could not stand alone.

You may have noticed from the above that there is another way of phrasing the indirect object. We have been saying that Sue gave a jumper **to** Oxfam. Thus:

(12)   Sue gave **Oxfam** a jumper

can also be phrased as:

(13)   Sue gave a jumper **to Oxfam**

Similarly:

(14)   Ray told **the children** a story

can also be phrased as:

(15)   Ray told a story **to the children**

To, you will remember, is a preposition and in these examples it has joined with the noun phrases *Oxfam* and *the children* to form prepositional phrases. So far we have only looked at prepositional phrases which function as adverbials. Here we are showing another function; that of indirect object. A constituent which **functions** as an **indirect object** then can have either the **form** of an **NP** (examples (12) and (14)) or the **form** of a **PP** (examples (13) and (15)).

The tree for a ditransitive verb incorporating a PP is:

(16a)

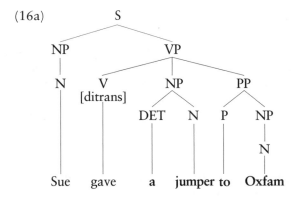

and the function of the constituent phrases is:

(16b) Sue   gave   a jumper   to Oxfam
        S   P   dO   iO

We can now change the 'rules to remember' for a prepositional phrase to incorporate this second type of function.

Rules to remember: Prepositional Phrase (PP)

PP → P (+ NP)

function: 1. *A*
        2. *iO*

e.g. 1. Sally looked **up**
      Sally looked **up the chimney**
    2. Sue gave a jumper **to Oxfam**

You may also have noticed that the direct and indirect objects occupy different positions in the sentence according to whether two noun phrases

(NP + NP) or a noun phrase and a prepositional phrase (NP + PP) are used. In the original example at (10) using NP + NP the sequence is:

(17)   *S*   *P*   *iO*   *dO*
       Sue   gave   **Oxfam**   **a jumper**

as opposed to:

(18)   *S*   *P*   *dO*   *iO*
       Sue   gave   **a jumper**   **to Oxfam**

In other words, if NP + NP is used, the indirect object precedes the direct object; if NP + PP is used then the direct object precedes the indirect object.

However, it does not mean that all verb phrases using the structure V + NP + PP are ditransitive. In a sentence such as:

(19)   Ken   made   a cake   for the party
              V   +   NP   +   PP

the prepositional phrase *for the party* is **not** functioning as an indirect object. You can test this by trying to substitute the alternative structure NP + NP (with the resultant switch in positions of *dO* and *iO*) as in:

(20)   *Ken   made   the party   a cake
              V   +   NP   +   NP

If the verb *made* was functioning as a ditransitive verb, this substitution should work, as in the alternative structures for *told* and *gave*, but it clearly does not. In the example at (19) the prepositional phrase is functioning as an adverbial, and as such it is optional.

(21a)

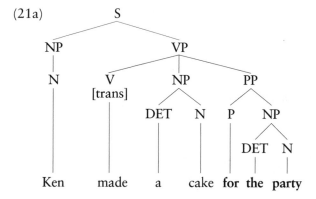

(21b) Ken   made   a cake **for the party**
      S   P   *dO*   **A**

Made is in this instance therefore a transitive verb with an obligatory noun phrase functioning as direct object and an optional prepositional phrase functioning as adverbial. Again these are differences between **form** and **function; form** is what a constituent **is** (e.g. NP, PP), **function** is what a constituent **does** (e.g. *dO, iO, A*). In this context, the form NP functions as direct object, the form PP functions as adverbial. In the context of a ditransitive verb using a PP (as in example 18)), the form NP again functions as direct object, but the form PP functions as indirect object.

Rules to remember: Ditransitive Verb

VP → ditransitive verb + *iO* + *dO*
iO → NP
dO → NP

e.g. Sue – **gave** – **Oxfam** – **a jumper**

OR

VP → ditransitive verb + *dO* + *iO*
dO → NP
iO → PP

e.g. Sue – **gave** – **a jumper** – **to Oxfam**

Exercise 8

Draw trees for the following sentences, classifying the verbs. (Check your analyses on pages 145–6.)

1. Sally showed the children the pictures
2. The children screamed hysterically
3. The baby loves this teddy
4. Ken gave the cake to the children
5. The children bought Ken a present
6. She patted the dog on the head

Now analyse the same sentences and the following set of sentences in terms of function.

7. Ken made a cake for the party
8. Ken made a cake for Sally
9. She wrote a letter to the council
10. She wrote a message on the wall

Intensive Verb

INTENSIVE VERBS (sometimes referred to as **relational, linking,** or **copular**) belong to a small group which include verbs like, *be* (most commonly), *seem, appear, become, look* and so on. What these verbs have in common is that what follows the verb in a sentence relates back to what precedes the verb (i.e. the noun-phrase subject). For example:

(22a)   Sally became **a doctor**
(22b)   George is **in the garden**
(22c)   Sue seems **unhappy**

In each of these examples what is given after the verb relates back to the subjects, describing their states. The bit that comes after the verb functions as the SUBJECT COMPLEMENT, shorthand version *sC*. Although the **functions** of all these bits are the same, the **forms**, as you may have noticed are different. In the first example, an NP functions as the *sC* (subject complement), and in the second, a PP functions as the *sC*. (22c) corresponds to a structure we looked at earlier when discussing the adjective phrase (AP) (pages 31–4). This example illustrates one function of the adjective phrase; that is, *sC* (subject complement). The intensive verbs are the only class of verb that can appear in the kind of construction at (22c), where the VP is completed by an AP alone.

We can now update the 'rules to remember' for adjective phrases and prepositional phrases to incorporate this *sC* function.

Rules to remember: Adjective Phrase (AP)

AP → (AdvP) + A

function: *sC*

e.g. Sue seems **unhappy**
     The dog is (**quite disgustingly**) **fat**

Rules to remember: Prepositional Phrase (PP)

PP → P (+ NP)

function: 1. *A*
         2. *iO*
         3. *sC*

e.g. 1. Sally looked **up**
      Sally looked **up the chimney**
   2. Sue gave a jumper **to Oxfam**
   3. George is **in the garden**

It is important to note that verbs in the **intensive** verb class, like transitive and ditransitive verbs, are incomplete on their own. In other words, some sort of *sC* is obligatory, as can be seen from:

(23a) *Sally became
(23b) *George is
(23c) *Sue seems

Whereas all (and only) intensive verbs can appear with just the category AP, the verb *be* is the only intensive verb which can appear with **any** of the categories at (22) (i.e. NP, PP, AP). For example, we can have:

(24a) Sally is **a doctor** (NP)
(24b) Sally is **in the garden** (PP)
(24c) Sally is **unhappy** (AP)

and we can have:

(25a) Sally became **a doctor** (NP)
(25b) Sally became **unhappy** (AP)

but not:

(26a) *Sally became **in the garden** (PP)

or:

(26b) *Sally seems **in the garden** (PP)

The tree diagrams for the examples at (22) are quite straightforward.

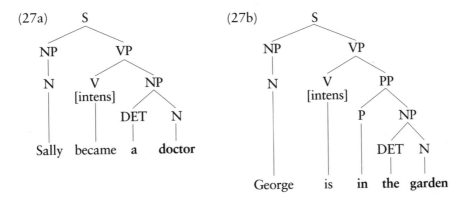

In terms of function the sentence patterns are the same.

(28a) Sally   became   **a doctor**
        S   P   sC
(28b) George   is   **in the garden**
        S   P   sC
(28c) Sue   seems   **unhappy**
        S   P   sC

Rules to remember: Intensive Verb

VP → intensive verb + sC
sC → NP or PP or AP

e.g. 1. Sally – is – **a doctor**
       2. George – is – **in the garden**
       3. Sue – seems – **unhappy**

Exercise 9

Draw tree diagrams for the following examples and analyse them in terms of
function. (Check your analyses on pages 145–8.)

1. That man is a teacher
2. The queen waved to the crowd
3. The crowd cheered
4. The statue is by the pond
5. She gave him a kiss
6. She rewarded him with a kiss
7. Sue paid the money to the cashier
8. The answer seems clear
9. George broke the statue
10. He laughed nervously

Complex-transitive Verb

Another class of verb to appear with a complement is called COMPLEX-
TRANSITIVE. With this type of verb the complement relates to the **object**,
not the **subject**. The complement is therefore an OBJECT COMPLEMENT
and the shorthand version is *oC*. For example:

(29a) The voters   elected   Mary   **president**
        S   *P*   *dO*   *oC*
(29b) Kate   thought   John   **a fool**
      S   *P*   *dO*   *oC*

With this type of verb, two elements are obligatory to complete the verb
phrase, in these cases, two noun phrases.
   The tree diagram for (29b) is:

(30)

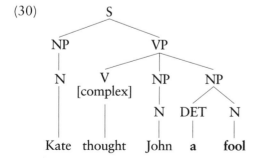

Some verbs can belong to more than one verb class. *Elected*, for instance, can also be classified as a transitive verb, as in:

(31)   The voters   elected   Mary
        S   *P*   *dO*

where it occurs simply with the direct object *Mary*. When it appears in a complex-transitive verb slot, however, an object complement (*oC*) is necessary (in example (29a), *president*, which relates back to *Mary*).

The structure of the sentence at (30) is also, you may have noticed, very similar to that given at (9a) to illustrate a ditransitive verb. That is, in both cases the verb phrase is completed by two consecutive NPs.

(9a)   Ray told   **the children**   **a story**
                 NP   +   **NP**
(30)   Kate thought   **John**   **a fool**
                 NP   +   **NP**

In (9a), though, the NPs are functioning respectively as *iO* (*the children*) and *dO* (*a story*). In (30) the functions are *dO* (*John*) and *oC* (*a fool*). So how can you tell the difference between the two types of verb? If you remember, one test for a ditransitive verb is the ability of the indirect object to take the form of either an **NP** or a **PP**. If a verb is ditransitive, then the noun phrase immediately following the verb functions as the *iO*. We can therefore try converting the noun phrases occupying that position in the above examples, to prepositional phrases.

(32a)   Ray told a story **to the children**
(32b)   *Kate thought a fool **to/for John**

Exercise 10

Try the above test with the following examples. Draw trees to indicate the verb classification and analyse in terms of function. (See analyses on page 149.)

1. The porter called George a taxi
2. The porter called George an idiot

An object complement can also take the form of a PP. For example:

(33a)   Carol   put   the car   **in the garage**
        S   *P*   *dO*   *oC*

(33b) George   stood   the lamp   **on the table**
      S   P   *dO*   *oC*

Both these verb phrases are incomplete without the second constituent, the PP:

(34a) *Carol put the car
(34b) *George stood the lamp

The tree diagram for (33a) is:

(35)

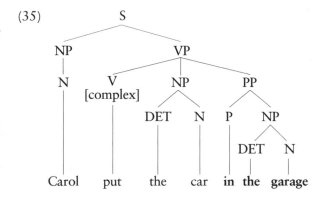

Again there is a similarity between a sentence with a complex-transitive verb and a following structure NP + PP, and a sentence with a ditransitive verb and a following structure NP + PP. What is the difference between these next examples?

(36a) Ken put the cake in the oven
(36b) She gave a bone to the dog

In the first example the prepositional phrase *in the oven* is an object complement (*oC*) and in the second, the PP *to the dog* is an indirect object (*iO*). How can you test for the difference? As before, a PP which functions as an *iO* should also be able to take the form of an NP. If you try it with the examples at (36) the results are:

(37a) *Ken put the oven the cake
(37b) She gave the dog a bone

Updating the 'rules to remember' for a prepositional phrase:

52 The Verb Phrase

Rules to remember: Prepositional Phrase (PP)

PP → P (+ NP)

function: 1. *A*
         2. *iO*
         3. *sC*
         4. *oC*

e.g. 1. Sally looked **up**
      Sally looked **up the chimney**
   2. Sue gave a jumper **to Oxfam**
   3. George is **in the garden**
   4. Carol put the car **in the garage**

Exercise 11

Draw trees for the examples at (36) showing the different verb classification and analysing in terms of function. Now try it with the following examples. (Check your analyses on pages 150–1.)

Ken offered the cake to Sally
Sue hung the washing on the line

The third category which can appear as an object complement (*oC*) is AP (adjective phrase), as in:

(38a) John made Kate **angry**
      S   *P*   *dO*   *oC*
(38b) Kate called John **stupid**
      S   *P*   *dO*   *oC*

Again the **object complement** (*oC*) refers to the **direct object** (*dO*) (in these cases *Kate* and *John*) and again **both** constituents are compulsory with a complex-transitive verb. The tree diagram for (38a) is as follows:

(39)

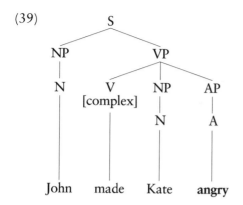

Updating the 'rules to remember' for an adjective phrase:

Rules to remember: Adjective Phrase (AP)

AP → (AdvP) + A

function: 1. *sC*
        2. *oC*

e.g. 1. Sue seems **unhappy**
     The dog is **(quite disgustingly) fat**
    2. John made Kate **angry**

Rules to remember: Complex-transitive Verb

VP → complex-transitive verb + *dO* + *oC*
dO → NP
oC → NP or PP or AP

e.g. Kate – **thought** – **John** – **a fool**
    Carol – **put** – **the car** – **in the garage**
    John – **made** – **Kate** – **angry**

Prepositional Verb

The last class of verb we will look at is the PREPOSITIONAL VERB. A prepositional verb is one which requires a prepositional phrase in order to be complete. Verbs like *glance*, *lean*, *refer*, fall into this class. In fact they are so closely linked with a preposition that it is easy to think of them as verbs consisting of two parts, as in *glance at*, *lean on*, *refer to*. They are certainly incomplete without a prepositional phrase as can be seen from:

(40a)   Sally leant on the table
(40b)   *Sally leant

(41a)   The children glanced at the pictures
(41b)   *The children glanced

The function of the prepositional phrase in this structure is PREPOSI-TIONAL OBJECT (*pO*). This adds another function to remember:

Rules to remember: Prepositional Phrase (PP)

PP → P (+ NP)

function: 1. *A*
         2. *iO*
         3. *sC*
         4. *oC*
         5. *pO*

e.g. 1. Sally looked **up**
       Sally looked **up the chimney**
   2. Sue gave a jumper **to Oxfam**
   3. George is **in the garden**
   4. Carol put the car **in the garage**
   5. The children glanced **at the pictures**

The tree diagram for (41a) is:

(42)

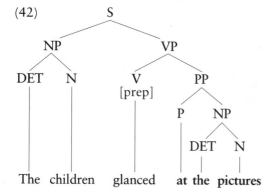

The children   glanced   **at the pictures**

and the function of the constituents:

(43)   The children   glanced   **at the pictures**
                S   P   *pO*

Rules to remember: Prepositional Verb

VP → prepositional verb + *pO*
pO → PP

e.g. The children – **glanced** – **at the pictures**

Exercise 12

Draw trees for the following examples and analyse them in terms of function.
(Check your analyses on pages 151–3.)

1. The baby played in the playpen
2. Kate dealt with the problems
3. Henry died in the night
4. The dog lay by the fire
5. Sally leant on the table
6. Sally danced on the table

Imperative

Most of the example sentences we have considered so far have been DECLARATIVES; that is, they make some kind of declaration or assertion. Being in the **declarative mood** they have followed the structure NP + VP, function *S – P*. The **imperative mood** differs from this in that it is used to give commands or instructions. Sentences in the imperative may omit the subject NP. For example:

(44)   Close the door!
(45)   Beat the eggs lightly

These examples use a different structure from those we have looked at so far and can be analysed:

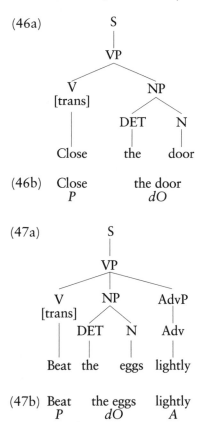

(46a)

(46b)   Close   the door
          P   *dO*

(47a)

(47b) Beat   the eggs   lightly
        P   *dO*   *A*

It is possible to give commands and instructions without using the imperative, for example:

(48)   Could you close the door?

can be, and probably usually is, interpreted as an instruction rather than a question.

The term **imperative** therefore refers to the **structure of the sentence** rather than its **function in conversation**.

Exercise 13

Analyse the following in terms of form and function. (Check your analyses on pages 153–8.)

1. Children hate the dark
2. The wind whistled through the trees
3. The medicine made her ill
4. She rode a donkey at the seaside
5. The wind blew
6. He put the cake in the oven
7. This verb is intensive
8. Shut that door
9. The doctor gave her the medicine
10. Hilary is a hairdresser
11. Actually she rode a donkey
12. The wind howled eerily
13. She gave the medicine to the baby
14. The boys called the girls names
15. The villa is near the beach
16. Obviously he relies on her

Summary of Rules

Verb Classes

Rules to remember: Complex-transitive Verb

VP → complex-transitive verb + *dO* + *oC*
dO → NP
oC → NP or PP or AP

e.g. Kate – **thought** – John – a fool
  Carol – **put** – the car – in the garage
  John – **made** – Kate – angry

Rules to remember: Ditransitive Verb

VP → distransitive verb + *iO* + *dO*
iO → NP
dO → NP

e.g. Sue – **gave** – Oxfam – a jumper

OR

VP → ditransitive verb + *dO* + *iO*
dO → NP
iO → PP

e.g. Sue – **gave** – a jumper – to Oxfam

Rules to remember: Intensive Verb

VP → intensive verb + *sC*
sC → NP or PP or AP

e.g. 1. Sally – **is** – a doctor
  2. George – **is** – in the garden
  3. Sue – **seems** – unhappy

Rules to remember: Intransitive Verb

VP → intransitive verb

e.g. Ken – **snores**

Rules to remember: Prepositional Verb

VP → prepositional verb + pO
pO → PP

e.g. The children – **glanced** – **at the pictures**

Rules to remember: Transitive Verb

VP → transitive verb + dO
dO → NP

e.g. Kate – **hugged** – **the baby**

Phrases

Rules to remember: Adjective Phrase (AP)

AP → (AdvP) + A

function: 1. sC
         2. oC

e.g. 1. Sue seems **unhappy**
    The dog is (**quite disgustingly**) **fat**
  2. John made Kate **angry**

Rules to remember: Prepositional Phrase (PP)

PP → P (+ NP)

function: 1. *A*
          2. *iO*
          3. *sC*
          4. *oC*
          5. *pO*

e.g. 1. Sally looked **up**
        Sally looked **up the chimney**
    2. Sue gave a jumper **to Oxfam**
    3. George is **in the garden**
    4. Carol put the car **in the garage**
    5. The children glanced **at the pictures**

4 The Verb Group

Although we have looked in some detail at the sort of constituents which appear with various classes of verb to complete the verb phrase, we have so far largely ignored the verb itself. All our examples have used a single verb as in *The dog **found** a bone*, *Jenny **hit** him* and so on. But verbs can consist of one or more than one element as in, for example:

(1a)   Kate **hugged** the baby
(1b)   Kate **was hugging** the baby
(1c)   Kate **has been hugging** the baby.

These elements, one or more than one, form the VERB GROUP (**Vgp**).

The verb groups in the examples at (1a–1c) have something in common in that they all include the verb *hug* in one form or another (i.e. *hugged*, *hugging*). This is the part of these verb groups which carries the meaning and is called the LEXICAL VERB (**V**). All complete verb groups **have** to include a lexical verb which appears last in the group and forms the HEAD of the verb group. The lexical verb can appear alone as in (1a) or with additional elements as in (1b) (*was*) and (1c) (*has been*). These additional elements are called AUXILIARIES (**AUX**) (*auxiliary* meaning *additional* or *giving help*). Auxiliary verbs **modify** the lexical verb by indicating MODALITY, or ASPECT or VOICE. In addition, the verb group may signify TENSE and for reasons given below, TENSE will also be included under the category **auxiliary**.

To describe the constituents of a sentence more accurately then, the tree diagrams should detail the verb group. In other words, a diagram should show that a verb phrase (VP) consists initially of a verb group (Vgp), and that the verb group consists of auxiliaries (AUX) and a lexical verb (V). For example, for a verb phrase incorporating a transitive verb we would have:

(2)   VP   →   verb group + *dO*
      Vgp   →   AUX + V
      dO   →   NP

Since the VP consists initially of a Vgp rather than just a lexical verb, it is the Vgp node which will indicate verb class. To see how this works we'll look in more detail at **tense, modality, aspect** and **voice**.

Tense

There are two tenses in English: PRESENT and PAST. (*Future* does not exist as a tense in English but is indicated in other ways, for example by use of auxiliaries.) These tenses affect the form of the lexical verb as in:

(3a)   Present tense
       Kate **hugs** the baby
(3b)   Past tense
       Kate **hugged** the baby

The verb *hug* is a **regular verb** in that it takes the ending *-ed* to form the past tense, as do many other verbs in English. **Irregular verbs** appear in a variety of forms. For example:

(4a)   The dog **eats** the bone
(4b)   The dog **ate** the bone

(5a)   She **is** hungry
(5b)   She **was** hungry

You can doubtless think of many others. In sentences such as those above, tense is signified by the form of the lexical verb. In more complex verb-group structures this is not the case. So that we can see how tense works more clearly, it is helpful to analyse it as part of the auxiliary group. By giving tense a node on the tree diagram, it is possible to separate it out from other elements in the verb group. For example:

(6a)

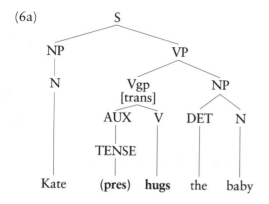

(6b)

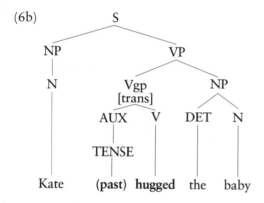

You can see from these diagrams how tense affects the form of the following verb; that is, it dictates the type of ending the next part of the verb group (in these cases the lexical verb) will have. Each constituent of AUX has the effect of dictating the ending of the following part of the verb group in a kind of knock-on effect. Tense is one part of this.

Exercise 14

Practise drawing tree diagrams incorporating Vgp for the examples at (4) and (5). (Check your analyses on pages 158–9.)

Modal Auxiliaries

Rather than expressing a statement of fact either present or past as in examples (6a) and (6b), MODALITY allow us to express whether a state of affairs is likely, possible, necessary and so on. A feature of the language which allows us such expression is the MODAL auxiliary (**MOD**). The modal auxiliaries are:

will, would, can, could, may, might, shall, should, must, ought to

and marginally:

need, dare, used to

Will and *would* signify volition or prediction as in:

(7a)   Kate **will** hug the baby
(7b)   The baby **would** like a hug

Can, could, may and *might* indicate possibility or probability as in:

(8a)   Kate **can** hug the baby
(8b)   Kate **could** hug the baby
(8c)   The baby **might** like a hug

Shall, should, must and *ought* signify obligation as in:

(9a)   Kate **should** hug the baby.
(9b)   The baby **must** want a hug

A modal auxiliary does not carry tense and is indicated on the tree diagram, immediately dominated by the AUX node as follows:

(10)

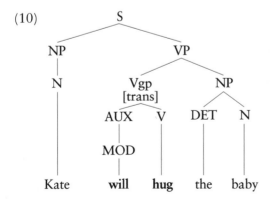

The form of the lexical verb *hug* is again different from those we looked at when considering tense ((6a) and (6b)). A verb group incorporating a modal auxiliary however has no tense so it is the modal auxiliary that has served to dictate the verb form *hug* in example (10). The form of the verb which appears after a modal is called the INFINITIVE. The infinitive carries no endings either for person (as in (*she*) *hug-s*) or for tense (as in *hugg-ed*). It can appear with the particle *to*, **to + infinitive**, as in *to hug*, or as a **bare infinitive** (without *to*) as in *hug*. It is the second form, the bare infinitive, that follows a modal. Most infinitive forms are fairly straightforward and can be arrived at either from the present- or past-tense forms. For example, *walk-s* or *walk-ed* become (*to*) *walk*. Others are a little less simple. For example, *find-s* becomes *found* in the past tense; the infinitive form is (*to*) *find*. Most notoriously irregular is the verb *to be*: its infinitive form doesn't appear again as part of the other forms.

A modal auxiliary then always appears with the infinitive form of the following verb (in (10) the lexical verb) and so we can find constructions like:

(11a)   The dog **found** a bone
(11b)   The dog **must find** a bone

(11c)   Jenny **hits** him
(11d)   Jenny **may hit** him

(11e)   The baby **cried** hourly
(11f)   The baby **might cry** hourly

and so on.

The function of the entire Vgp is that of Predicator (*P*). That is:

(12a)   Kate   (**pres**) **hugs**   the baby
        S   P   dO
(12b)   Kate   **will hug**   the baby
        S   P   dO
(12c)   The baby   (**past**) **cried**   hourly
        S   P   A
(12d)   The baby   **will cry**   hourly
        S   P   A

Rules to remember: Auxiliaries – modals

1. Modal auxiliary + infinitive

e.g. **will**   **hug**

Exercise 15

Draw the tree diagrams for the sentences at (11a) to (11f) incorporating Vgp analysis. (Check your analyses on pages 160–1.)

Primary Auxiliaries

Auxiliary verbs which are not modals are called PRIMARY auxiliaries. These are:

have, be, do

For now we'll restrict our attention to *have* and *be* and the way these two signify **aspect** and **voice**.

The meaning of the term **aspect** is not easy to define but has to do with time and the relationship of actions or states to periods of time or duration. It is much easier to define aspect in terms of its **formal features** (i.e. the **form** the verb group takes to signify aspect). There are two kinds of aspect: PERFECT and PROGRESSIVE.

Perfect Aspect

Perfect aspect (**PERF**) is indicated by the presence of the auxiliary verb *have*. For example:

(13a)   Sally **has** finished this book
(13b)   Sue **had** given the dog a bone.

Unlike the **modal** auxiliaries, the **primary** auxiliaries do carry tense. In a verb group without a modal, it is always the first element which is marked for tense; that is the element immediately following TENSE. If therefore there is only one element in the verb group (i.e. the lexical verb (V)) this must show tense, as in the example at (3b), *Kate hugged the baby*. If there is a primary auxiliary verb as in (13a) and (13b), then as the first element in the verb group it is the auxiliary which carries the tense. Example (13a) is present tense (*has*), (13b) is past tense (*had*).

The tree diagram showing the verb group incorporating TENSE and the perfect auxiliary (PERF) is:

(14)

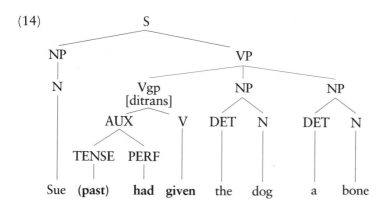

You can see from this diagram that TENSE (past) has dictated the form of the following verb, the auxiliary *have*, realizing *had*. The perfect auxiliary *have* similarly dictates the form of the verb which follows it, in this case the lexical verb *give*. The form of the verb which always follows the perfect auxiliary is called the PAST PARTICIPLE. It is important to remember, however, that the *past* in *past participle* does not refer to tense (which can be present as in (13a)) but to the form of the verb. As far as the verb *finish* is concerned ((13a)), the past-participle form is realized in the same way as the past-tense form, by the addition of *-ed*, as it is for many other verbs. *Give*, however, is an irregular verb with a past-tense form *gave* and a past-participle form *given*. Because of these irregular verbs, the past-participle form is also referred to as the *-en* form. This distinguishes it from the regular *-ed* past-tense form.

Again, the function of the entire Vgp is Predicator (*P*).

(15)   Sue   (past) had given   the dog   a bone
       S   *P*   *iO*   *dO*

Rules to remember: Auxiliaries – perfect aspect

2. Perfect aspect: *have* + *-en* form
                              (past participle)

    e.g. **had**   **given**

Exercise 16

Draw the tree diagrams for the following examples and analyse in terms of function. (Check your analyses on pages 162–4.)

1. Sally has finished this book
2. George had been in the garden
3. The guests had gone by midnight
4. The dog has eaten the bone
5. That letter might arrive in the morning
6. The phone rings continually
7. Jack sat in the corner
8. Ken can cook the dinner

The modal auxiliary can also combine with the perfect, in which case tense cannot feature. Although different types of auxiliary may appear together, each type can only appear once in any verb-group structure. For example a modal auxiliary (MOD) plus perfect aspect (PERF) plus the lexical verb (V) could produce:

(16)
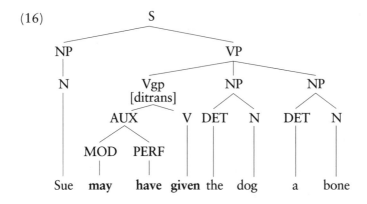

Notice that the modal auxiliary *may* is followed by the infinitive *have*. (If you remember, modals are always followed by infinitives.) The perfect auxiliary *have* is followed by the *-en* (or past-particle) form *given*. In this way each element of the verb group dictates the shape or form of the following one.

You may also notice that the auxiliaries appear in a fixed order. We have already said that the lexical verb is always last (in this case *given*) but it is also the case that when both modal and perfect auxiliaries are used, the modal always precedes the perfect. You can test this by trying it out the other way around as in:

(17)   *Sue **have may given** the dog a bone

Exercise 17

Analyse the following in terms of form and function. (Check your analyses on pages 164–6.)

1. This example should have been illuminating
2. She may have put the food in the cupboard
3. He could have taken the money
4. The penny dropped
5. Sally has written an article
6. She might write a book

Progressive Aspect

The other kind of aspect is called **progressive** aspect (**PROG**) and this is indicated by the presence of the auxiliary verb *be*. For example:

(18a)   Sally **is** walking along the beach.
(18b)   Sue **was** giving the dog a bone.

The tree diagram incorporating the verb group and the progressive auxiliary is:

(19)

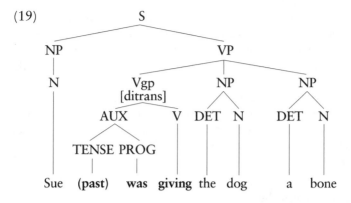

Again the tense is shown on the first element in the verb group; present tense *is* in (18a) and past tense *was* in (18b).

The form of the verb which follows the progressive auxiliary is called the PRESENT PARTICIPLE. It is easy to spot as it is the *-ing* form of the verb.

Rules to remember: Auxiliaries – progressive aspect

3. Progressive aspect: *be* + *-ing* form
                                   (present participle)

      e.g.   **was giving**

The progressive can also combine with modal and/or perfect auxiliaries. Again, each type of auxiliary may appear only once in the verb group and if modal appears, then tense cannot. For example:

(20)   modal + progressive + V
       Sue **may be giving** the dog a bone

(21)   present tense + perfect + progressive + V
       Sue **has been giving** the dog a bone

(22)   modal + perfect + progressive + V
       Sue **may have been giving** the dog a bone.

As ever, the modals are followed by infinitives; perfect aspect is followed by the *-en* form of the verb; progressive aspect is followed by the *-ing* form of the verb. Tense falls on the first element of the verb group (unless a modal auxiliary is used).

No matter what combination of auxiliary verbs you may have, they will always appear in the same set order. That is, tense or modal (if used) precedes both perfect (if used) and progressive (if used); perfect (if used) precedes progressive (if used). They all precede the lexical verb. That is:

Vgp → AUX + LEXICAL VERB
AUX → tense/modal (+ perfect) (+ progressive)

Exercise 18

Draw the tree diagrams for the following and analyse in terms of function. (Check your analyses on pages 166–8.)

1. Sally is walking along the beach
2. Sue may be giving the dog a bone
3. Sue has been giving the dog a bone
4. Sue may have been giving the dog a bone
5. The students are revolting

Then, using the modal *must* where modal is indicated, construct the verb groups for the following.

Example: (She) modal + *run* = (She) must run

  6. (She) modal + perfect + *run*
  7. (She) past tense + perfect + progressive + *run*
  8. (She) modal + progressive + *run*
  9. (She) present tense + progressive + *run*
10. (She) modal + perfect + progressive + *run*
11. (She) past tense + *run*
12. (She) present tense + perfect + *run*

Passive Voice

A final feature to consider in verb groups is that of **voice**. Voice refers to whether a sentence or utterance is in the ACTIVE or the PASSIVE. All our examples so far have been active. The majority of sentences and utterances are in the active and so this feature is not overtly marked on a tree diagram.

Let's look again at an earlier example of an active sentence:

(23)

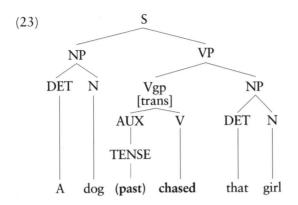

You will remember that we said that the subject of a sentence is that NP which is immediately dominated by S; the object is that NP which is immediately dominated by VP. In the above sentence then *a dog* is the subject; *that girl* is the object. These terms *subject* and *object* refer to the grammatical relations holding between constituents and have to do with sentence position. In order to explain the passive, we will look at the semantic relations of these constituents. (Remember semantics is the study of meaning.) In (23), *a dog* is not only the grammatical subject of the sentence but is also the **agent** of the action. That is, the dog is not only the focus of our attention, or what is being talked about, but it is also the character doing the chasing. Similarly, *that girl* is not only the grammatical object of the verb *chased*, she is also the character being chased or acted upon; she has the role of **affected**. To change this sentence from active to passive we first switch the positions of agent and affected:

(24a)   **That girl** chased **a dog**

Clearly though this has changed the meaning. In order to retain the original meaning (i.e. that the dog was doing the chasing (agent), the girl was being chased (affected)) the verb group has to be modified:

(24b)   That girl **was chased** a dog

Finally, the noun phrase *a dog* becomes a prepositional phrase:

(24c)   That girl was chased **by a dog**

All this may seem fairly complicated and you should remember that passives are in a minority. However, they do have their uses. For example, in passive sentences, specifying agent is optional, which may be quite handy as in, for instance:

(25a) Active
       I committed a heinous crime last night
(25b) Passive
       A heinous crime **was committed** last night **(by me)**

As far as the verb group is concerned, you will be able to see that the passive (**PASS**) is signified within the verb group by the presence of the verb *be*. Since in the examples at (24c) and (25b) this is the first element of the verb group, tense is shown on this element (i.e. past in both cases). When it is acting as a passive auxiliary, the verb *be* is followed by the past participle or *-en* form. This differentiates it from *be* acting as a progressive auxiliary when it is followed by the present participle or *-ing* form. On the tree diagram, the passive is shown as:

(26)

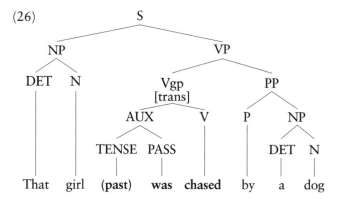

You can see from the tree that the affected, *that girl*, now appears in the subject position (i.e. the NP node immediately dominated by S); the agent is still *a dog* but this noun phrase now follows the verb as part of a prepositional phrase, *by a dog* (functioning as adverbial (*A*)).

As far as grammatical relations are concerned, it is the noun phrase which filled the direct-object slot which now appears in the subject position. It is therefore only those verbs which are otherwise incomplete without a grammatical object that allow for the passive structure, that is, transitive, ditransitive, complex-transitive and prepositional.

> **Rules to remember: Auxiliaries – passive voice**
>
> 4. Passive voice: *be* + *-en* form
>   (past participle)
>
>   e.g.   **was chased**

Passives can also appear with other auxiliaries. So, for example we could have

(27)   modal + passive + V
       The dog **may be given** a bone (by Sue)

(28)   present tense + perfect + passive + V
       The dog **has been given** a bone (by Sue)

(29)   present tense + progressive + passive + V
       The dog **is being given** a bone (by Sue)

and so on. All combinations are possible but it is important to remember that the order is still fixed with passive now coming after tense/modal, perfect and progressive, and that each auxiliary dictates the form of the following verb, be it another auxiliary or the lexical verb.

Vgp → AUX + LEXICAL VERB
AUX → tense/modal (+ perfect) (+ progressive) (+ passive)

It is possible to use all the auxiliary verbs together:

(30)

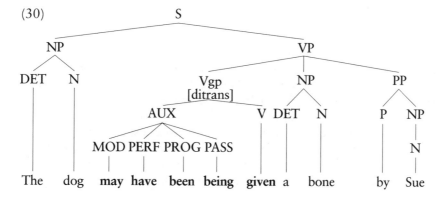

This unlikely and somewhat cumbersome sentence at least serves to illustrate the order in which the auxiliary verbs appear. That is:

Rules to remember: Order of Auxiliaries

1. Tense or
       modal + infinitive
2. Perfect: *have* + *-en*
3. Progressive: *be* + *-ing*
4. Passive: *be* + *-en*

   + LEXICAL VERB

Exercise 19

Analyse the following in terms of form and function. (Check your analyses on pages 169–70.)

1. The dog had been given a bone
2. A bone has been given to the dog
3. The murder was committed by the butler
4. He must have been arrested
5. She is shocked by the news

Using the modal *must* where modal is indicated, construct the verb groups for the following:

Example: (She) past tense + passive + *see* = (She) **was seen**

  6. (She) modal + perfect + passive + *see*
  7. (She) modal + perfect + *see*
  8. (She) past tense + progressive + passive + *see*
  9. (She) present tense + perfect + *see*
10. (She) past tense + *see*

Do

The primary auxiliary we have not considered so far is *do*. Do turns up to lend support to the lexical verb only in certain constructions and where there is no other auxiliary verb already present. For example you can make a straightforward statement like:

(31)   I like bananas

but in order to make the same statement negative the verb requires *do* support, as in:

(32)   I **do** not like bananas

(or *I don't like bananas*). If one of the other auxiliaries is already present, this process is not needed, as in:

(33a)   You **must** eat bananas
(33b)   You **must not** eat bananas

Again, if you want to question the statement at (31), *do* is necessary in the absence of another auxiliary verb as in:

(34)   **Do** you like bananas?

but not in:

(35a)   You **must** eat bananas
(35b)   **Must** you eat bananas?

You can also see that, for questions, the auxiliary verb (*do* in (34) and *must* in (35)) and the subject *you* change places in the sentence.

Another function for *do* as an auxiliary is to provide emphasis. For example:

(36)   You **do** like bananas.

Do as an auxiliary is the first constituent of the verb group and therefore carries tense:

(37)

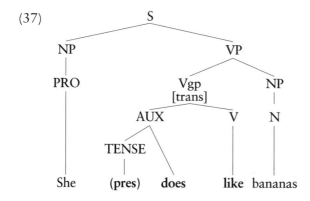

Do when it appears as an auxiliary is followed by a bare infinitive.

Rules to remember: Auxiliary *do*

do + infinitive

Exercise 20

Analyse the following sentences in terms of both form and function. (Check your analyses on pages 171–4.)

1. He may have said something
2. She might be seen by the neighbours
3. George has been drinking
4. George does drink heavily
5. Ray had been telling the children a story
6. She must be innocent
7. Ken is being stopped by the police
8. Sally must have thought George an idiot
9. Sue has been visiting the theatre regularly
10. The attic is visited by a ghost
11. The summons might have been delivered already

Summary of Rules

Rules to remember: Auxiliaries – modals

1.   Modal auxiliary + infinitive

e.g. **will**   **hug**

Rules to remember: Auxiliaries – perfect aspect

2. Perfect aspect: *have* + *-en* form
                              (past participle)

e.g.   **had   given**

Rules to remember: Auxiliaries – progressive aspect

3. Progressive aspect: *be* + *-ing* form
                              (present participle)

e.g.   **was giving**

Rules to remember: Auxiliaries – passive voice

4. Passive voice: *be* + *-en* form
                              (past participle)

e.g.   **was   chased**

Rules to remember: Order of auxiliaries

1. Tense or
     modal + infinitive
2. Perfect: *have* + *-en*
3. Progressive: *be* + *-ing*
4. Passive: *be* + *-en*
     + LEXICAL VERB

Rules to remember: Auxiliary *do*

do + infinitive

5   The Noun Phrase

In the example sentences we have used so far the noun phrases have mainly been simple, consisting of either DET + N, or just N. The quick introduction to adjectives and adjective phrases in chapter 2 (pp. 31–4) though indicates that a noun phrase can contain other elements within it. We can now look at the possible constituents of the noun phrase in more detail.

We said earlier that the most meaningful part of a noun phrase is the noun. It is the obligatory constituent and is the HEAD of the noun phrase. There are different types of noun; we have already mentioned **common**, **proper** and **abstract** nouns. We also said that a noun phrase could consist of a PRONOUN and this is the category we will look at in most detail in the next section.

Pronouns

Examples of pronouns we have used so far include *you*, *he*, *her*, as in:

(1)   **He** chased **her**
(2)   **You** must eat bananas

These are examples of PERSONAL PRONOUNS. The personal pronouns are:

1st person singular	*I/me*	1st personal plural	*we/us*
2nd person singular	*you*	2nd personal plural	*you*
3rd person singular	*she/her*	3rd personal plural	*they/them*
	he/him		
	it		

Personal pronouns refer to specific entities. To say or write:

(3) **She** loves football

is to refer to a specific *she*, and one who we presume the hearer or reader can identify.

Unlike the nouns in noun phrases, some of the personal pronouns have different forms according to their sentence position. For example the nouns in the following two examples are the same in either position:

(4) **Girls** hate **boys**
(5) **Boys** hate **girls**

Compare the above to the following personal pronouns:

(6) **I** hit **her**
(7) **She** hit **me**
(8) **We** smiled at **him**
(9) **He** smiled at **us**

In (6)–(9) the form of the pronoun changes according to whether it is in subject position or not.

You may remember that one of the tests for categorizing a noun phrase is the ability to replace it with a pronoun. So, for instance:

(10) **A dog** chased **that girl**

can become:

(11) **It** chased **her**

and:

(12) **Girls** hate **boys**

can become:

(13) **They** hate **them**

Other groups of pronouns are:

INDEFINITE (referring to unspecified entities): *some, something, anything, anyone, someone*

(14)   **Some** like it hot
(15)   **Anything** goes

DEMONSTRATIVE: *this, that, these, those*

(16)   **This** is really pretty
(17)   **That** is very ugly

INTERROGATIVE: *who, which, what, whose*

(18)   **Who** is coming to dinner?
(19)   **Which** is the train to Ipswich?

POSSESSIVE: *mine, yours, hers, ours, yours* (plural), *theirs*

(20)   The red book is **mine**
(21)   **Yours** is on the table

REFLEXIVE: *myself, yourself, herself, himself, itself, ourselves, your-selves, themselves*

(22)   Ken loves **himself**
(23)   The children hurt **themselves**

As is customary we have been marking the presence of a pronoun in tree diagrams. The shorthand version is **PRO.** For example:

(24a)

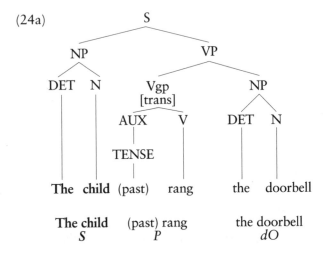

(24b)

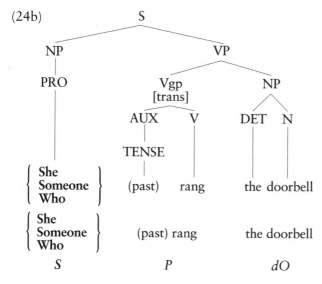

Pre- and Post-modification

Noun phrases, then, can consist of one constituent, the **head** (e.g. PRO), or more than one constituent (e.g. DET + N). Where other constituents do exist, they form part of the noun phrase and are said to **modify** the head noun. Constituents which modify the head noun can appear before it or after it. Those which appear **before** the head noun are called PRE-MODIFIERS; those which appear **after** the head noun are called POST-MODIFIERS. We will look at pre-modifiers first.

Pre-modification

Constituents which pre-modify nouns are **determiners (DET)**, **adjective phrases (AP)**, and **nouns**.

Determiners

We have already looked at the basic determiners (page 6), which are the **indefinite article**, *a/an* and the **definite article**, *the*. Other determiners are:

DEMONSTRATIVES: *this, that, these, those*
QUANTIFIERS: *some, any, each, every, no,* etc.
POSSESSIVES: *my, your, her, his, its, our, your* (plural), *their*
WH-DETERMINERS: *whose, what, which*

Some of these determiners appear to be the same or similar to some of the pronouns listed above (for example, the demonstratives). Sort out the difference between them in the following examples:

Some like it hot
Some people like it hot
My book is on the table
The red book is mine
This jumper is very colourful
This is really pretty
Which is the train to Ipswich?
Which train goes to Ipswich?

You should have noticed that pronouns appear on their own to form the noun phrase; determiners appear with a head noun.

Genitives

Apart from the list above, the possessive determiner can also be realized as a phrase, for example:

(25a)   **This boy's** clothes are incredibly dirty
(25b)   **Kate's** baby is crying

where there is an NP (*this boy, Kate*) + *'s*. These possessive phrases (**POSS**) or **genitives** take the sentence position normally occupied by the determiner as in:

(26a) $\left\{ \begin{array}{l} \textbf{The} \\ \textbf{This boy's} \end{array} \right\}$ clothes are incredibly dirty

(26b) $\left\{ \begin{array}{l} \textbf{The} \\ \textbf{Kate's} \end{array} \right\}$ baby is crying

This being the case, we will analyse it as a determiner as follows:

(27a)

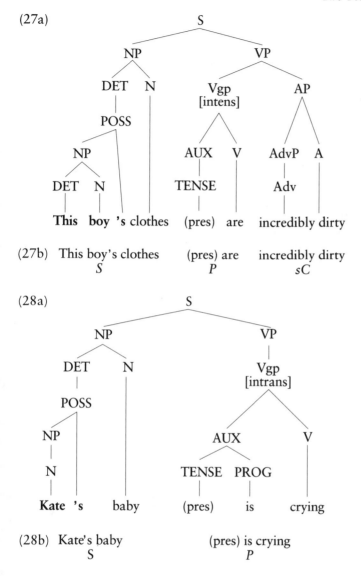

(27b)   This boy's clothes   (pres) are   incredibly dirty
       S   P   sC

(28a)

(28b)   Kate's baby   (pres) is crying
      S   P

Adjective Phrases (AP)

Adjective phrases (AP) are also used to **pre-modify** nouns. We looked briefly at the constitution of adjective phrases earlier (pages 31–4). Using the example we used then, we said that *the dog* in *The dog chased a girl* could also be *the fat dog*. The adjective *fat* slots in between the determiner *(the)* and the noun *(dog)* so that the noun phrase is expanded. That is:

(29a) **The dog**   chased a girl
(29b) **The fat dog** chased a girl

Remember that an adjective phrase, like any other phrase, can consist of one or more than one element (e.g. *fat, very fat*). Within the NP, then, the AP has the function of **pre-modifying** the head. However, when analysing function we will continue to label only the higher level sentence function of the entire NP, in this case either *the dog* or *the fat dog*. In the sentences at (29) these noun phrases are the subjects and the entire noun phrase with or without a pre-modifying adjective phrase is analysed as such.

To see how this works, substitute a pronoun for the noun phrase. Using the pronoun *it* for the subject, see what it replaces in (29a) and (29b).

In (29a) *it* replaces *the dog* and in (29b) *it* replaces *the fat dog*. So the function analysis for (29a) and (29b) is the same. That is:

(30) ⎧ **The dog**   ⎫
     ⎨ **The fat dog** ⎬   chased a girl
     ⎩ **It**   ⎭
              S   P   dO

Now the question arises of how this new-look noun phrase is analysed in terms of its constituent parts and how it appears on a tree diagram. One possibility is:

(31a)

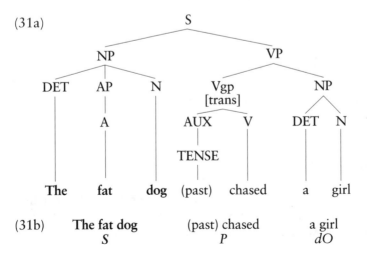

(31b)   **The fat dog**   (past) chased   a girl
                 S   P   dO

You will remember though that one of the reasons we had for forming individual constituents into phrases was that they seemed to belong closely together (as with DET and N, for example). One way we have of testing this is to substitute a pronoun, as we have just done, to see what is replaced. In the above examples, ((29) and (30)) this showed us that the three constituents determiner, adjective phrase and noun all belonged together to form one phrase, the noun phrase.

However, it is also the case that *fat* and *dog* seem to belong together more closely than *the* and *fat* or *the* and *dog*. Perhaps then the two constituents AP and N form a separate phrasal constituent at a lower level within the NP. We can test this suggestion by using a WH-determiner to question the statement at (29b) as follows:

(32a)   Which **fat dog** chased a girl?
(32b)   That   **one**   (= that **fat dog**)

In the answer at (32b), the determiner *that* replaces the determiner *which*, but the term *one* replaces not just *dog*, but *fat dog*. So the three elements *which* + *fat* + *dog* have been replaced by two, *that* + *one*. The need for the determiner remains constant but because the two elements *fat* and *dog* can be replaced by one element (i.e. *one*), this means that they function together at this level as a single unit or constituent. If two elements function as one constituent, they should have their own exclusive node within the tree. In the above diagram, the elements *fat* and *dog* do not have such a node. They are both dominated by the NP node but this is not exclusive since it also includes DET. We must therefore create a system which shows not only that the three elements *the* + *fat* + *dog* form one constituent (that is, dominated by the NP node), but that the elements *fat* + *dog* also form a complete constituent within that larger one. What we can do then is to break the subject noun phrase down as follows:

(33)

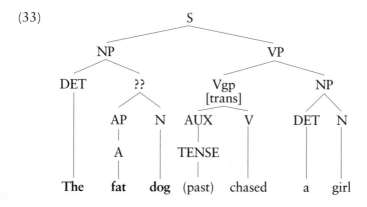

This shows us that the entire noun phrase *the fat dog* is one constituent (replaceable by *it*) and that there is another constituent, *fat + dog* (replaceable by *one*), within it. The problem then arises as to what this constituent *fat + dog* should be called. It is not a full NP since it doesn't contain a determiner, neither is it simply a noun (N). The constituent therefore has to be given another label. One solution to the problem is to use a label from a theory of syntax called X-bar theory and call this constituent N-bar (written N′). It is not necessary to go into the details of X-bar theory here, but we will borrow the label N′ which will signify that this is an intermediate constituent, smaller than an NP but larger than an N. The tree at (33) then becomes:

(34)

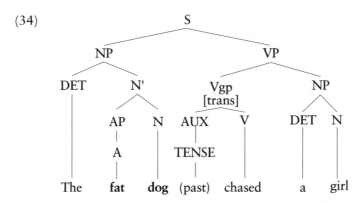

Noun phrases can contain more than one adjective as the earlier example *the fat brown dog* indicates. That is:

(35)   **The fat brown dog** chased a girl

In the same way that *the dog* in example (29a), and *the fat dog* in example (29b) form one noun phrase, so too does *the fat brown dog*, even though it has more constituent parts. Try again the substitution test by replacing the subject noun phrase in (35) with the pronoun *it*.

We now have to work out how to show this noun phrase on the tree diagram and will start by looking at the question:

(36)   Do you like this **fat brown dog** or that **thin one**?

Do you understand *one* in this question to mean *dog* or **brown dog**? If you understand it to mean the latter then *one* is replacing *brown + dog*, in which case these two elements form one unit. Again, this unit is smaller than an NP, but larger than an N, so is labelled N'. This is represented on the tree diagram for (35) below:

(37)

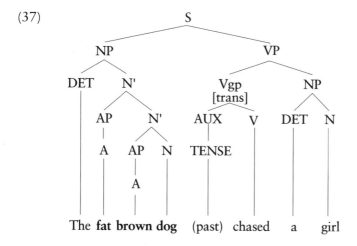

For present purposes we will follow this interpretation and use the structure at (37).

We can now update the rules for adjective phrases:

Rules to remember: Adjective Phrases (AP)

AP → (AdvP) + A

function: 1. *sC*
        2. *oC*

e.g. 1. The dog is (**quite disgustingly**) **fat**
    2. John made Kate **angry**

OR

function: pre-modifier within NP

e.g. The **fat brown** dog chased a girl

Exercise 21

Draw trees for the following and analyse in terms of function. (Check your analyses on pages 175–7.)

1. The red hen ate her corn
2. The quick brown fox jumped over the lazy dog
3. Sue's dog seems remarkably happy
4. The time has come for a huge celebration
5. Those unhappy students might have failed their final exams
6. This hateful child has given my best coat to Oxfam

Nouns

Nouns also serve to **pre-modify** other nouns. For example:

(38)   I bought a new **computer** game
(39)   The **electricity** board sent her a nasty letter

In cases such as these, the noun pre-modifier is so closely connected to the head noun that the two can almost be considered one word. This close link is illustrated by the fact that when nouns do pre-modify other nouns they always come next to the head noun; nothing else can come between them:

(40)   *I bought a computer new game

The analysis should reflect the fact that the noun pre-modifier and the head noun are so closely linked. We can do this by including them both under the name N node:

(41)

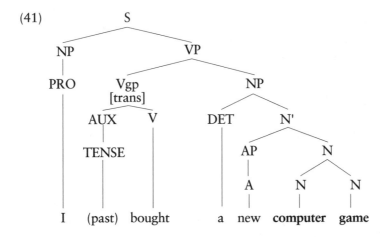

Exercise 22

Draw tree diagrams for the following and analyse in terms of function. (Check your analyses on page 178.)

1. The electricity board sent her a nasty letter
2. This is a tree diagram
3. My younger sister might become a taxi driver

Post-modification

As stated before, constituents which **modify** the head noun can also appear after the noun. Such constituents are **post-modifiers**. Here we will look at two ways to post-modify a noun:

PREPOSITIONAL PHRASE: e.g. The dog chased the cat **with three legs**
RELATIVE CLAUSE: e.g. The cat **which is lying on the mat** hates dogs

We will look at these in turn.

Prepositional Phrase (PP)

We have already looked at prepositional phrases (PP) with regard to other functions; that is, as adverbials and as indirect objects. Now we come to a further function; that of **post-modifying** the head noun in a noun phrase.
    Take the example above:

(42)   The dog   chased   the cat with three legs
          S   *P*   *dO*

Just as an adjective before the noun, the prepositional phrase after the noun is acting to modify the noun by more narrowly defining or describing it. The prepositional phrase belongs closely to *the cat* and forms part of the noun phrase. Its function within the noun phrase is to post-modify the head noun; at a higher level, the function of the entire noun phrase (including the prepositional phrase) is that of direct object of the sentence. We can check that the prepositional phrase forms part of the noun phrase by again substituting the pronoun *it* for the direct object of the sentence at (42):

(43)   The dog chased **it**

As you can see, *it* has replaced the entire expression *the cat with three legs*, not just *the cat*.

Compare this to a sentence where a prepositional phrase is functioning as an adverbial:

(44)   The dog   chased   the cat   **up the tree**
        S   *P*   *dO*   *A*

If we use the pronoun *it* to replace the direct object in this sentence we get:

(45)   The dog chased **it** up the tree

Here *it* has only replaced the expression *the cat*. In this example, *the cat* and *up the tree* are separate constituents.

Another way to check this is to move the direct-object NPs in each example to the subject position (as in the passive):

(46)   **The cat with three legs** was chased (by the dog)
(47)   **The cat** was chased up the tree (by the dog)

In (46) it is the determiner and noun (*the cat*) plus the prepositional phrase which moves to subject position thereby functioning as one unit. In (47) it is only the noun phrase *the cat* which moves, leaving the separate PP constituent behind.

Again we have to consider the tree analysis for this type of NP. If we look solely at the noun phrase *the cat with three legs* we could suggest an analysis of:

(48)

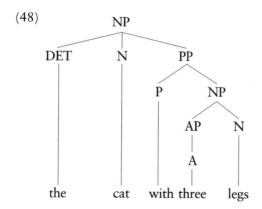

This though runs into the same type of problem that we had with adjective phrases in that if we ask the question:

(49)   Do you prefer this **cat with three legs** or that **one**

the need for a determiner remains constant but the term *one* is understood as replacing *cat with three legs*, not just *cat*. The phrase *cat with three legs* must then function at this level as a constituent separate from DET and the tree diagram should show this, as below:

(50a)

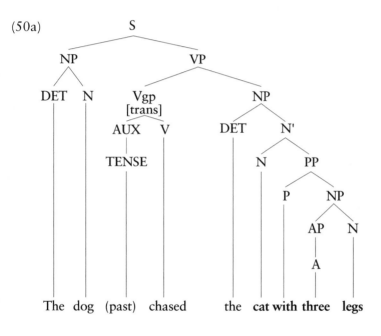

(50b) The dog   (past) chased   the cat with three legs
        S   P   dO

The intermediate constituent *cat with three legs* is again labelled N' to indicate that it is smaller than NP but larger than N.
    Compare (50a) to the tree diagram for (44):

(51a)

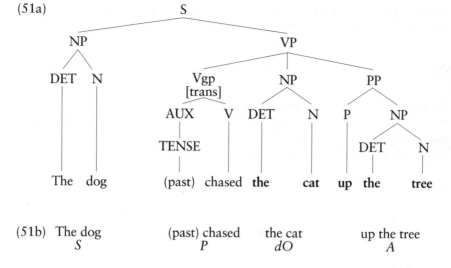

(51b) The dog   (past) chased   the cat   up the tree
       S   *P*   *dO*   *A*

Again we can update the rules for a prepositional phrase to include this function:

Rules to remember: Prepositional Phrase (PP)

PP → P (+ NP)

function: 1. *A*
          2. *iO*
          3. *sC*
          4. *oC*
          5. *pO*

e.g. 1. Sally looked **up**
       Sally looked **up the chimney**
    2. Sue gave a jumper **to Oxfam**
    3. George is **in the garden**
    4. Carol put the car **in the garage**
    5. The children glanced **at the pictures**

OR

function: post-modifier within NP

e.g. The dog chased the cat **with three legs**

Exercise 23

Draw tree diagrams for the following showing the difference between a PP post-modifying an NP and a PP functioning as adverbial. (Check your analyses on pages 179–82.)

1. Life is a bowl of cherries
2. The man with the wooden leg walked slowly
3. The man walked along the road
4. The old woman hit the man with the wooden leg
5. The dog bit the old man on the nose
6. The woman on the bus was telling me the story of her life

Relative clause

A **relative clause** is a bit different from anything we've looked at so far because it introduces a kind of subsidiary sentence into the main one. For example:

(52)   The cat **which is lying on the mat** loves dogs

If we take the relative clause out of the above example, you can see that it almost forms another S in its own right:

(53a)

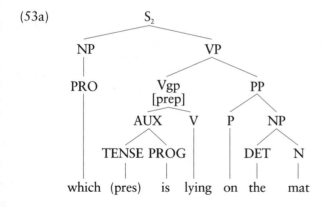

(53b)   which   (pres) is lying   on the mat
          S   P   pO

Which in the above example is a RELATIVE PRONOUN, so called because it stands in place of and **relates** to *the cat*. Other relative pronouns are *who* as in:

(54)   The girl **who** was chased by the dog was crying

and *that*, as in:

(55)   He kicked a can **that** was lying in the road.

Although we have extracted the example at (53) from the full sentence at (52), it doesn't quite form an S on its own because it doesn't really make sense on its own. You can't, for instance, just say 'Which was lying on the mat' in isolation. On the other hand, the part of the sentence which is left when (53) has been extracted, **does** make sense on its own.
That is:

(56)   The cat loves dogs

There seem to be then two Ss in the example at (52); one more complete than the other. The one that is more complete (i.e. *the cat loves dogs*) is called the MAIN CLAUSE (S_1). The other chunk (i.e. *which is lying on the mat*) is a SUBORDINATE CLAUSE (S_2). In this case the type of **subordinate clause** is a **relative clause**. (There are other types of subordinate clause which we will come to later (pp. 101–20).) The point about a relative clause is that it **functions to post-modify a head noun**, in this case *the cat*. As with our other examples of post-modifiers, this means that the NP *the cat* and the relative clause *which is lying on the mat* both function together at a higher level as one constituent; the subject NP of the sentence. Again you can test that this is one constituent by substituting a pronoun:

(57a)   It loves dogs
(57b)   *It which is lying on the mat loves dogs

The tree diagram is as follows:

(58a)

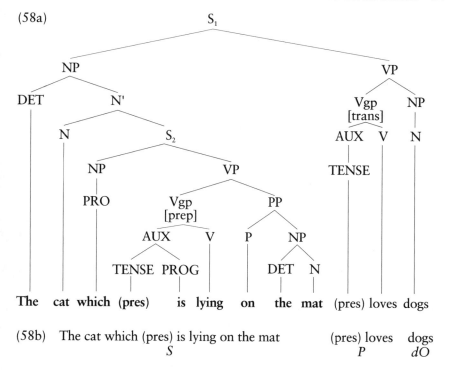

(58b)   The cat which (pres) is lying on the mat   (pres) loves   dogs
                                        S   P   dO

Again, *cat which is lying on the mat* is also analysed as one constituent (N′) because it can be replaced by *one*, as in:

(59)   Do you prefer this **cat which is lying on the mat** or that **one**?

Although the subordinate relative clause (S₂) has been analysed here in terms of its constituent parts, we will in future be considering these and other types of subordinate clause in their entirety, that is, as whole units. When a constituent is being considered as a whole unit and not in terms of its individual components it is notated on the tree diagram by a triangle, thus:

(60)

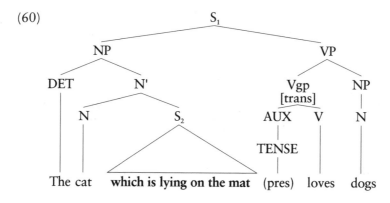

The cat   **which is lying on the mat**   (pres)   loves   dogs

---

Rules to remember: Noun Phrase (NP)

NP → (pre-modifiers) + HEAD (+ post-modifiers)

pre-modifiers → DET   e.g. **a** game
                AP   e.g. a **new** game
                N   e.g. a new **computer** game

post-modifiers → PP   e.g. the cat **with three legs**
                 Rel clause (S)   e.g. the cat **which is lying on the mat**

Exercise 24

Using triangle notation, draw tree diagrams for the following sentences and analyse them in terms of function. (Check your analyses on pages 182–6.)

1. The face that launched a thousand ships was amazingly beautiful
2. The spy who loved me has gone
3. She collected the letters that were lying on the table
4. The typist copied the letter on her pad
5. The typist copied the letter in her own time
6. I found her a reliable typist
7. I found him a reliable typewriter
8. The lame dog that is following me might be lost

Summary of Rules

Rules to remember: Adjective Phrases (AP)

AP → (AdvP) + A

function: 1. *Sc*
          2. *oC*

e.g. 1. The dog is (**quite disgustingly fat**)
      2. John made Kate **angry**

OR

function: pre-modifier within NP

e.g. The **fat brown** dog chased a girl

Rules to remember: Noun Phrase (NP)

NP → (pre-modifiers) + HEAD (+ post-modifiers)

pre-modifiers → DET   e.g. **a** game
               AP   e.g. a **new** game
               N   e.g. a new **computer** game

post-modifiers → PP   e.g. the cat **with three legs**
                 Rel clause (S) e.g. the cat **which is lying on the mat**

Rules to remember: Prepositional Phrase (PP)

PP → P (+ NP)

functions: 1. *A*
         2. *iO*
         3. *sC*
         4. *oC*
         5. *pO*

e.g. 1. Sally looked **up**
       Sally looked **up the chimney**
   2. Sue gave a jumper to **Oxfam**
   3. George is **in the garden**
   4. Carol put the car **in the garage**
   5. The children glanced **at the pictures**

OR

function: post-modifier within NP

e.g. The dog chased the cat **with three legs**

6 Subordination and Coordination

We saw in chapter 5 (pp. 95–8) that it is possible to have more than one S node in a sentence. The example we looked at earlier, *the cat which is lying on the mat loves dogs*, was seen to consist of a MAIN CLAUSE (S_1) (*the cat loves dogs*) and a SUBORDINATE CLAUSE (S_2) (*which is lying on the mat*). S, then, is more accurately described as shorthand for **clause** rather than for sentence. A clause may exist alone or it may join up with other clauses (as in example (60) page 98). One way of joining clauses together is to SUBORDINATE one to another; another way is to COORDINATE them. A style of speech or writing using lots of subordination is called HYPOTACTIC; a style using little subordination is called PARATACTIC. Following on from the last chapter, we will look at subordination first.

Subordination

Most of our example sentences so far have consisted of one clause. That is, we have taken different subjects and said one thing about them in each sentence. For example:

(1)   Kate hugged the baby
(2)   Jenny hit me
(3)   The dog found a bone

We can, of course, take the same subject and say different things about it in different sentences:

(4)   The cat is mad
(5)   The cat loves dogs

Alternatively we can join the clauses together to form one sentence. As we said above, one way to do this is to subordinate one clause to another. For example:

(6)   The cat that is mad loves dogs

In example (6), *the cat loves dogs* becomes the **main clause**; *that is mad* is the **subordinate clause** introduced by a SUBORDINATOR, the relative pronoun *that*. These two clauses do not carry equal weight or importance: the **subordinate clause** is often less important than the **main clause**. Alternatively we could subordinate (5) to (4):

(7)   The cat that loves dogs is mad

In this example, the assertion *the cat loves dogs* has become less important than the assertion *the cat is mad*. In other words, (4) has become the **main clause** and (5) has become the **subordinate clause**. Material in a subordinate clause can often be deleted if necessary, for example when summarizing information.

   The tree diagram for (7) is similar to the one used for the earlier example of a subordinate clause (page 98). That is:

(8)

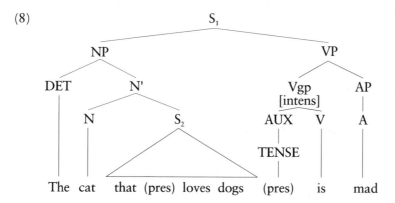

You can see clearly from its position on the tree that S_2 is further down the hierarchy than S_1. In other words, S_2 is dominated by S_1 and therefore subordinate to it.

There are various types of subordinate clause which we'll look at individually.

Relative Clause

The example at (8) is another example of a **relative clause**. You will remember that we said that a **relative clause post-modifies the head noun of a noun phrase** (see pages 95–6). In this case the relative clause is *that loves dogs* and it post-modifies the noun *cat*. The whole unit *the cat that loves dogs* is a noun phrase, functioning as the subject of the sentence. You can check that it is functioning as one constituent by substituting the pronoun *it*. (See also the discussion on page 97.) At the level of the whole sentence then the function analysis is:

(9)   The cat that loves dogs (pres) is   mad
          S   P   sC

We can also say that the subordinate clause *that loves dogs* is EMBEDDED in the main clause *the cat is mad*. One advantage of the tree diagram is that it shows this embedding quite clearly; in the example at (8), S_2 is contained or **embedded** in S_1.

This embedding is a feature of all subordinate clauses. For instance, in example (6), *the cat is mad* is the subordinate clause, *the cat loves dogs* is the main clause. This is analysed as:

(10)

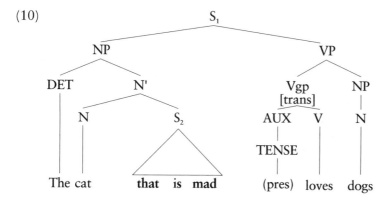

Again you can see from the diagram that S_2 is dominated by S_1 and subordinate to it. It is also embedded within S_1. As before, the triangle notation is used to show that a constituent is being considered in its entirety and that it is not necessary for current purposes to analyse it further.

Another way of showing embedding without the elaboration of a tree diagram is by the use of square brackets. For example:

(11)   [$_{S_1}$ The cat [$_{S_2}$ that is mad] loves dogs]

One feature of relative clauses is that it is not necessary in every case for them to be introduced by a subordinator; this can be optional. For example:

(12a)   [$_{S_1}$ The film [$_{S_2}$ **that I saw last night**] was really good]
(12b)   [$_{S_1}$ The film [$_{S_2}$ **I saw last night**] was really good]

As far as function is concerned, within the overall structure a relative clause always forms part of a larger NP and so takes on the function of that NP. For example:

(13) $\left\{ \begin{array}{l} \textbf{The cat that is mad} \\ \textbf{It} \end{array} \right\}$ (pres) loves   dogs

               S   P   dO

(14)   I   (pres) like $\left\{ \begin{array}{l} \textbf{the cat that loves dogs} \\ \textbf{it} \end{array} \right\}$

     S   P   dO

Exercise 25

The following contain examples of relative clauses post-modifying nouns. Using triangle notation, draw tree diagrams for these sentences and analyse them in terms of function. (Check your analyses on pages 186–8.)

1. Ken gave the cake that he made to Sally
2. Sally enjoyed the cake that Ken made
3. Sue's dog might have buried the bone she gave him
4. I like the dress you're wearing
5. The dress that Sally wore was a great success

Adverbial Clause

Like adverbs and adverb phrases, subordinate **adverbial clauses** add information in relation to manner, time, place and so on. They tend to answer the questions 'How?', 'When?', 'Where?', 'Why?' For example:

(15) I'll give you the next clue **when you're ready**
(16) We must be careful **because there's a ghost**
(17) **If I open this,** you can put the cake mix into the bowl

All adverbial clauses begin with a **subordinator**. In example (15) the subordinator is *when*; in examples (16) and (17) it is *because* and *if* respectively. There is no option to omit the subordinator in adverbial clauses (unlike the example of a relative clause we looked at earlier).

The tree diagram for the example at (15) is:

(18)

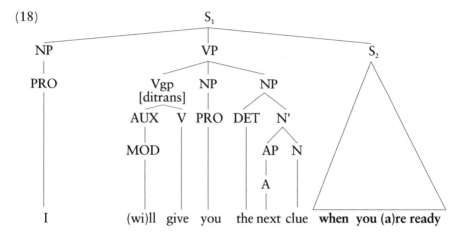

Adverbial clauses, like sentence adverbs, can appear in different sentence positions. For example, (15) could equally well be written as follows:

(19) $[_{S_1} [_{S_2}$**When you're ready**] I'll give you the next clue]

For this reason, the subordinate clause (S_2) is analysed as being immediately dominated by S_1 and not VP.

The function of subordinate adverbial clauses is, not surprisingly, adverbial.

(20) I   (wi)ll give   you   the next clue   **when you (a)re ready**
      S   P   iO   dO   *A*

Exercise 26

The following are examples of subordinate adverbial clauses. Using triangle notation, analyse these sentences in terms of form and function. (Check your analyses on pages 188–9.)

1. We must be careful because there's a ghost
2. When the lights are red you must stop
3. If I open this you can put the cake mix into the bowl

Noun Clause

In some cases it is possible for clauses rather than phrases to function as subjects or objects. These types of clause are called **noun clauses**. For example:

(21)   **How he deals with the deficit** is grossly important
(22)   I know **(that) they like me**
(23)   We told her **(that) she could come**

In (21) the subordinate clause is the subject, in (22) the subordinate clause is the direct object of a transitive verb, and in (23) the subordinate clause is the direct object of a ditransitive verb. These functions are indicated on the tree diagram: a subordinate clause functioning as a subject is immediately dominated by S_1 and a subordinate clause functioning as direct object is immediately dominated by VP. For example:

(24a)

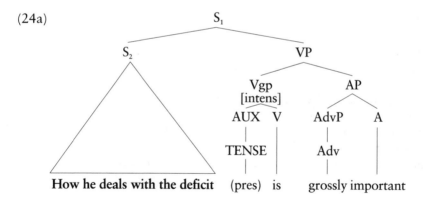

(24b) **How he deals with the deficit**   (pres) is   grossly important
         S   *P*   *sC*

You can check that the entire S_2 is functioning as the subject by substituting the pronoun *it*:

(25a)

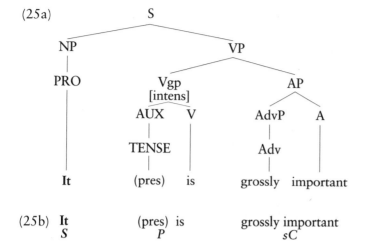

(25b)   **It**   (pres) is   grossly important
         S   P   sC

Similarly, a direct object:

(26a)

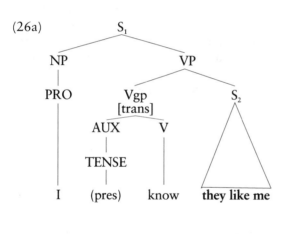

(26b)   I   (pres) know   **they like me**
         S   P   *dO*

Compares with:

(27a)

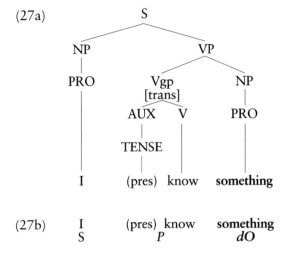

```
                           S
               _____/ _____
              NP                        VP
              |                    _____/ \_____
             PRO                 Vgp            NP
                                [trans]         |
                              __/    \__        PRO
                             AUX       V         |
                              |                  |
                            TENSE                |
                                                 |
              I            (pres)  know      something
```

(27b)   I   (pres) know   something
         S   P   *dO*

You can see from examples (22) and (23) that, as with some relative clauses, the subordinator is not always essential.

Because a noun clause functions as an obligatory element in a sentence, that is as a subject or an object, the main clause cannot stand independently on its own. This is different from the main clauses in sentences containing a subordinate relative or adverbial clause. For example, we said that in:

(28)   [s₁ The cat [s₂ that loves dogs] is mad]

the main clause is:

(29)   The cat is mad
         S   P   sC

This is complete, with subject, predicator and subject complement. Similarly, in:

(30)   [s₁ I'll give you the next clue [s₂ when you're ready]]

the main clause is:

(31)   I   (wi)ll give   you   the next clue
       S   P   iO   dO

which is again complete with subject, predicator, and both objects. In (24) though, the subordinate clause functions as subject so the main clause is incomplete:

(32)   [[S$_2$] **is grossly important**]

In (26) the subordinate clause functions as direct object, so again the main clause is incomplete:

(33)   [**I know** [S$_2$]]

Exercise 27

Using triangle notation, analyse the following in terms of form and function. What kind of subordinate clause is present in each example? (Check your analyses on pages 189–92.)

1. I chose this option because I love grammar
2. We thought that we were looking for a dark passage
3. They're the only ones I've got
4. What has been done already has been done extremely badly
5. We told her she could come
6. I love it when my plans work
7. What the election might bring is a change of leadership

Complement Clause

Subject complement

A subordinate clause can also appear with an intensive verb and function as the subject complement. For example:

(34a)   The important thing (pres) is **that you're happy**
                   S   *P*   *sC*

(34b)

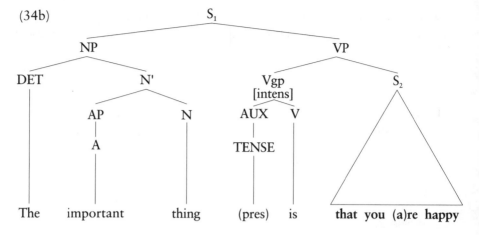

This presents a very similar situation to the one described above where a subordinate noun clause acts as direct object. The subordinate clause is functioning as an obligatory part of the sentence, so the main clause appears incomplete:

(35)   [**The most important thing is** [S₂]]

Complement of A

Subordinate clauses can also complement adjectives. For example:

(36)   I am **sure that she must have known him**
(37)   He made her **sorry that she knew him**

In both cases the subordinate clause forms part of the adjective phrase and takes on the same function within the sentence. That is:

(38a)

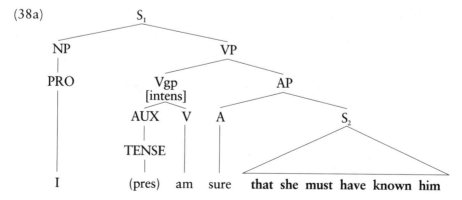

(38b)   I   (pres) am   **sure that she must have known him**
        S   P   **sC**

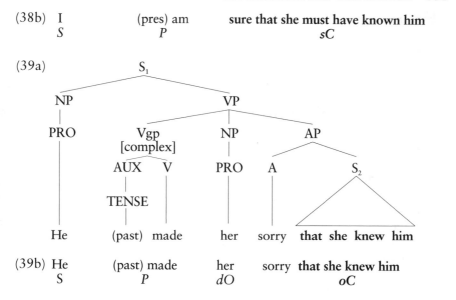

(39a)

```
                        S₁
          ┌──────────────┴───────────────┐
         NP                              VP
          │              ┌────────────────┴──────────┐
         PRO            Vgp              NP           AP
                      [complex]          │         ┌──┴────┐
                     ┌────┴───┐         PRO        A       S₂
                    AUX       V          │         │      ╱╲
                     │                   │         │     ╱  ╲
                   TENSE                 │         │    ╱    ╲
                     │                   │         │   ╱_____╲
         He       (past)  made          her      sorry  that she knew him
```

(39b)   He   (past) made   her   sorry **that she knew him**
        S   P   dO   **oC**

Exercise 28

Draw tree diagrams for the following and analyse in terms of function. Indicate the type of subordinate clause present in each. (Check your analyses on pages 192–3.)

1. She will be pleased that she came
2. I think she will be pleased
3. The chances are that she will be pleased

Non-finite Verbs

So far we have only looked at FINITE clauses; that is clauses where the verbs carry **tense.** There are occasions when NON-FINITE or **untensed** verbs can appear in subordinate clauses. The form of non-finite verbs is either *to* + **infinitive, bare infinitive** (that is infinitive without *to*), or the *-ing* and *-en* particles. Examples are:

to + **infinitive:**

(40)   She wants **to hold** the baby

bare infinitive:

(41)   She made him **hold** the baby

-ing **participle:**

(42)   She left him **holding** the baby

and *-en* participle:

(43)   **Bored** by the baby, she left

As with finite verbs, some non-finite verb groups can also be more complex. For example:

to + **infinitive**

(44)   perfect + *-en*
She wants **to have held** the baby
(45)   progressive + *-ing*
She wants **to be holding** the baby
(46)   passive + *-en*
The baby wants **to be held**

-ing **participle**

(47)   perfect + *-en*
She left happy **having held** the baby all day
(48)   perfect + *-en*; passive + *-en*
Having been held all day the baby slept peacefully

Analysing *to* as a **particle (part)**, the non-finite verb groups for examples (44)–(48) are:

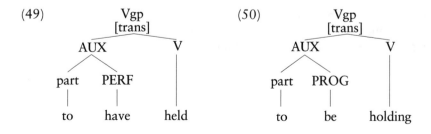

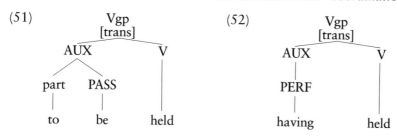

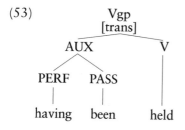

By definition, these verb groups cannot carry tense.

Also like finite subordinate clauses, non-finite clauses serve a variety of functions. We will look at those you are already familiar with.

Post-modifier

Like relative clauses, non-finite clauses can function as post-modifiers to head nouns (see pages 95–8 and 103–4). For example:

(54)   [$_{S_1}$ The letter [$_{S_2}$ **for you to type**] is on your desk]

The form of this non-finite verb is *to* + infinitive (*to type*) and by post-modifying *letter*, it forms part of the subject NP. As before, you can check that this is part of the subject NP by substituting the pronoun *it* for the subject of the sentence:

(55) $\begin{cases} \textbf{The letter for you to type} \\ \textbf{It} \end{cases}$ (pres) is on your desk

                          S   P   sC

We can analyse this as follows:

(56)

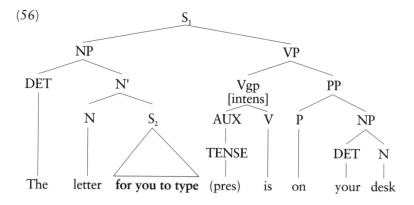

As with the other noun post-modifiers (PP and relative clause, see pages 93 and 97–8) we are arguing that *letter for you to type* is an N' constituent. You can check this with the *one* test we used earlier.

In the example at (56) the subordinator *for* is used. In other types of sentence construction using the non-finite *to* + infinitive a subordinator is not necessary.

(57a) [s₁ The letter [s₂ **to type**] is on your desk]
(57b) Passive + *-en*
          [s₁ The letter [s₂ **to be typed**] is on your desk]

Head nouns can also be post-modified by the *-ing* and *-en* participles. For example:

(58) The cat **lying** on the doorstep is asleep
(59) Those books **scattered** over the floor are yours

Again, you can test that these phrases are post-modifying the head nouns (*cat* and *books*) and are therefore part of the subject noun phrase by substituting a pronoun.

(60) **It** is asleep
(61) **They** are yours

The tree diagram for (58) is:

(62a)

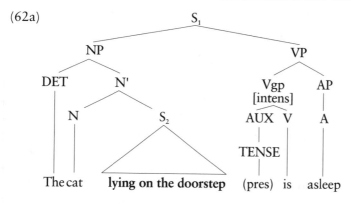

(62b)   The cat lying on the doorstep   (pres) is   asleep
                        S   P   sC

Again, *cat lying on the doorstep* forms an N' constituent.

Exercise 29

Draw tree diagrams for the following and analyse in terms of function. (Check your analyses on pages 193–6.)

1. I have nothing to wear
2. The food to be cooked is in the fridge
3. That man must have money to burn
4. That man is standing at the checkout
5. That man standing at the checkout has forgotten his money
6. Those books scattered over the floor are yours
7. The woman arrested for his murder was innocent
8. That little girl is wearing a red dress
9. The little girl wearing the red dress is Sally's daughter

We can now add the non-finite clause to the rules to remember for a noun phrase:

Rules to remember: Noun Phrase (NP)

NP → (pre-modifiers) + HEAD (+ post-modifiers)

pre-modifiers → DET   e.g. a game
             AP   e.g. a **new** game
             N   e.g. a new **computer** game

post-modifiers → PP   e.g. the cat **with three legs**
               Rel clause (S)   e.g. the cat **which is lying on the mat**
               Non-finite clause (S) e.g. the letter **for you to type** is on your desk
                                   the cat **lying on the doorstep** is asleep

---

Adverbial

Non-finite clauses can also function as adverbials (see pages 104–6). For example, *-ing* participle:

(63a)

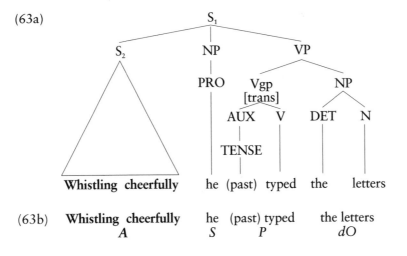

(63b)   **Whistling cheerfully**   he (past) typed   the letters
                A   *S*   *P*   *dO*

Again, because the adverbial can appear in more than one position (we could just as easily have *he typed the letters whistling cheerfully*), the subordinate clause is in this instance shown as immediately dominated by S_1. Adverbial non-finite clauses also appear in other forms. For example:

(64) *to* + infinitive

[s₁[s₂ [**To type the letters accurately**] he worked hard]

(65) *-en* participle

[s₁[s₂ [**Exhausted by his efforts**] he left early]

Exercise 30

Draw tree diagrams for the following and analyse in terms of function. (Check your analyses on pages 197–8.)

1. To type the letters accurately he worked hard
2. She might give him more letters to type
3. Exhausted by his efforts he left early
4. Reeling drunkenly they staggered from the pub
5. They must have had lots to drink

Subject

Like noun clauses (see pages 106–9), non-finite clauses can also appear as subjects:

(66a)

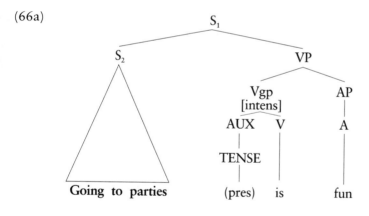

(66b) **Going to parties**   (pres) is   fun
              S   P   sC

You can check that S₂ is in fact the subject by substituting the pronoun *it*. That is:

(67) $\left\{ \begin{array}{l} \textbf{Going to parties} \\ \textbf{It} \end{array} \right\}$ is fun

In the example at (66), S_2 has no subordinator, but a subordinator may appear in a non-finite clause using *to* + infinitive. For example:

(68a)

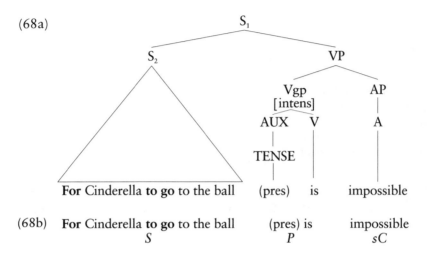

(68b)   **For** Cinderella **to go** to the ball   (pres) is   impossible
                                    S   *P*   *sC*

Direct object

Non-finite clauses, like noun clauses, can also function as direct objects (see pages 106–9).

(69a)

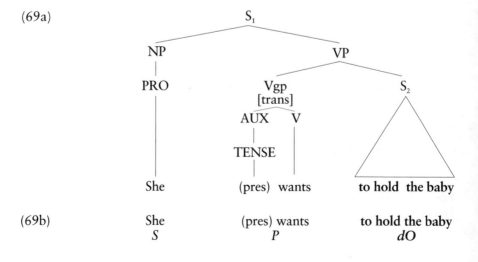

(69b)   She   (pres) wants   **to hold the baby**
                     S   *P*   *dO*

Once more, you can check that this is the direct object by substituting a pronoun:

(70)   She wants $\begin{Bmatrix} \text{something} \\ \text{to hold the baby} \end{Bmatrix}$

As with the noun clause, when a non-finite clause functions as a subject or object, it seems that the main clause is incomplete. (See the discussion on pages 108–9.) So, for example, the main clause in (69) is:

(71)   [**She wants** [S$_2$]]

This analysis can also be used for examples such as:

(72)   [$_{S_1}$ She wants [$_{S_2}$ **him to hold the baby**]]

for examples where a **bare infinitive** is used:

(73)   [$_{S_1}$ She made [$_{S_2}$ **him hold the baby**]]

and for examples where an *-ing* participle is used:

(74)   [$_{S_1}$ She likes [$_{S_2}$ **holding the baby**]]

Exercise 31

Draw tree diagrams for the following and analyse in terms of function. (Check your analyses on pages 198–201.)

1. To type accurately is difficult
2. They might like to take a winter break
3. Throwing tantrums is the story of her life
4. The passage for you to read can be found on the last page
5. Those students must enjoy going to lectures
6. Impressed with the meal they gave the waiter a large tip

Complement of A

The last function we'll look at is that of complementing adjectives. As with finite clauses (see pages 110–11), the subordinate non-finite clause functioning as complement of A forms part of the adjective phrase. For example:

(75)   Finite clause
        [She made him **sorry** [**that he went**]]
(76a)   Non-finite clause
        [She made him **sorry** [**to go**]]

(76b)

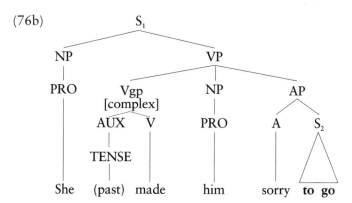

Since the subordinate clause is part of the AP, it has the same sentence function, in this case, object complement:

(76c)   She   (past) made   him   **sorry to go**
         S   P   dO   oC

Coordination

An alternative way of joining clauses together is to **coordinate** them. Coordinated elements are of equal importance and carry equal weight. One way of linking clauses in this way is to use the COORDINATOR (coord) *and*. For example:

(77)   My brother's got a little honey bear **and** it's china **and** he keeps honey
        in it

You can link as many clauses together as you like in this way, without ever making any one clause subordinate to another. They are all therefore **main clauses**. Other **coordinators** are *but* and *or*. An example of a tree diagram for coordinated clauses is as follows:

(78)

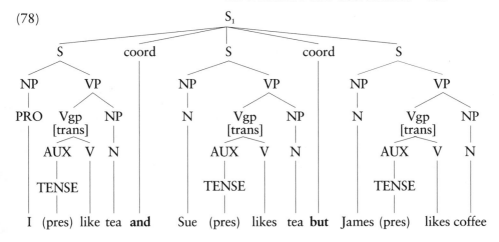

It is possible to coordinate phrases as well as clauses. For example:

(79)

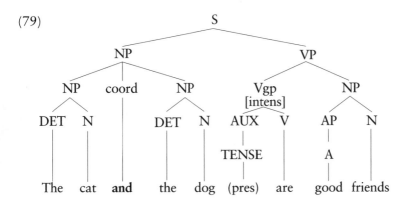

Both noun phrases *the cat* and *the dog* have equal importance; they are the joint subject of the sentence.

(80) The cat and the dog (pres) are good friends
       S   P   sC

You can test that this is so by substituting the plural pronoun *they* for the subject NP.

The example at (79) seems fairly straightforward. However, when noun phrases are pre-modified by adjective phrases the position is not quite so clear. For example, if we say:

(81)   Old women and men love cakes

do we mean that old women and all men love cakes, or that old women and old men love cakes? In other words, does the expression *old* refer to just *women* or to *men* as well? If it refers to just *women* then *old women* should have its own exclusive node on the tree diagram. The structure will therefore look like:

(82)

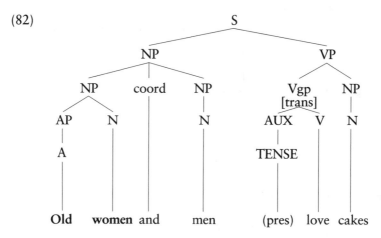

On the other hand if *old* refers to *men* as well as *women* then the structure will look like:

(83)

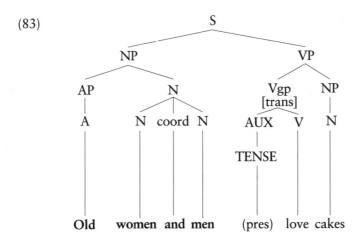

The sentence at (81) is ambiguous. Tree diagrams both illustrate and remove this ambiguity. The different structures at (82) and (83) indicate clearly how the sentence is to be interpreted.

Exercise 32

Draw tree diagrams for the following and analyse in terms of function. (Check your analyses on pages 201–5.)

 1. The dog ran across the road and the man chased it
 2. Sally is buying a new dress to wear for the party
 3. I like Jane but I hate her brother
 4. She might have been persuaded by the saleswoman
 5. Smoking cigarettes is a dangerous pastime
 6. Her ambition is to live a life of luxury
 7. Put those books on the table
 8. The books on the table are yours
 9. The waiter must have been certain that the bill was right
10. When I was four I said I was going on the stage

Summary of Rules

Rules to remember: Noun Phrase (NP)

NP → (pre-modifiers) + HEAD (+ post-modifiers)

pre-modifiers → DET   e.g. **a** game
                AP   e.g. a **new** game
                N   e.g. a new **computer** game

post-modifiers → PP   e.g. the cat **with three legs**
                  Rel clause (S)   e.g. the cat **which is lying on the mat**
                  Non-finite clause (S) e.g. the letters **for you to type** are on the desk
                                            the cat **lying on the doorstep** is asleep

---

Summary of All Rules

Phrases

Rules to Remember: Adjective Phrases (AP)

AP → (AdvP) + A

function: 1. *s*C
          2. *o*C

e.g. 1. The dog is (**quite disgustingly**) **fat**
     2. John made Kate **angry**

OR

Function: pre-modifier within NP

e.g. The **fat brown** dog chased a girl

Rules to remember: Adverb Phrase (AdvP)

AdvP → (deg) + Adv

function: *A*

e.g. Ken snores (**very**) **loudly**

Rules to remember: Noun Phrase (NP)

NP → (pre-modifiers) + HEAD (+ post-modifiers)

pre-modifiers → DET   e.g. **a** game
      AP   e.g. a **new** game
      N   e.g. a new **computer** game

post-modifers → PP   e.g. the cat **with three legs**
      Rel clause (S)   e.g. the cat **which is lying on**
                the mat
      Non-finite clause (S) e.g. the letter **for you to type**
              is on your desk
              the cat **lying on the**
              doorstep is asleep

Rules to remember: Prepositional Phrase (PP)

PP → P (+ NP)

function: 1. *A*
      2. *iO*
      3. *sC*
      4. *oC*
      5. *pO*

e.g.   1. Sally looked **up**
     Sally looked **up the chimney**
    2. Sue gave a jumper to **Oxfam**
    3. George is **in the garden**
    4. Carol put the car **in the garage**
    5. The children glanced **at the pictures**

OR

function: post-modifier within NP

e.g. The dog chased the cat **with three legs**

Verb Classes

Rules to remember: Complex-transitive Verb

VP → complex-transitive verb + dO + oC
dO → NP
oC → NP or PP or AP

e.g. Kate – **thought** – John – **a fool**
Carol – **put** – the car – **in the garage**
John – **made** – Kate – **angry**

Rules to remember: Ditransitive Verb

VP → ditransitive verb + iO + dO
iO → NP
dO → NP

e.g. Sue – **gave** – **Oxfam** – **a jumper**

OR

VP → ditransitive verb + dO + iO
dO → NP
iO → PP

e.g. Sue – **gave** – **a jumper** – **to Oxfam**

Rules to remember: Intensive Verb

VP → intensive verb + sC
sC → NP or PP or AP

e.g. 1. Sally – **is** – **a doctor**
2. George – **is** – **in the garden**
3. Sue – **seems** – **unhappy**

Rules to remember: Intransitive Verb

VP → intransitive verb

e.g. Ken – **snores**

Rules to remember: Prepositional Verb

VP → prepositional verb + *p*O
*p*O → PP

e.g. The children – **glanced** – **at the pictures**

Rules to remember: Transitive Verb

VP → transitive verb + *d*O
*d*O → NP

e.g. Kate – **hugged** – **the baby**

Auxiliary Verbs

Rules to remember: Auxiliaries – modals

1. Modal auxiliary + infinitive
e.g. **will**   **hug**

Rules to remember: Auxiliaries – perfect aspect

2. Perfect aspect: *have* + *-en* form
(past particiciple)

e.g. **had**   **given**

Rules to remember: Auxiliaries – progressive aspect

3. Progressive aspect: *be* + *-ing* form
(present participle)

e.g.   **was   giving**

Rules to remember: Auxiliaries – passive voice

4. Passive voice: *be* + *-en* form
(past participle)

e.g.   **was   chased**

Rules to remember: Order of Auxiliaries

1. Tense or
modal + infinitive
2. Perfect: *have* + *-en*
3. Progressive: *be* + *-ing*
4. Passive: be + *-en*

+ LEXICAL VERB

Rules to remember: Auxiliary *do*

do + infinitive

Answers to Exercises

Exercise 1 (page 13)

1.

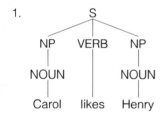

2.

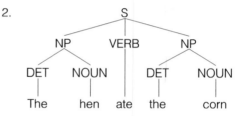

3.

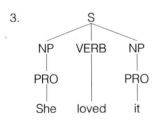

4.

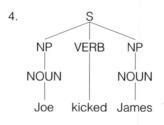

5.

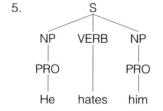

6.

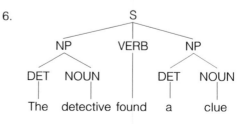

Exercise 2 (page 21)

Example sentences using the rules at (50) are:

a.   S → NP + VP

```
        S
       / \
      NP   VP
```

VP → V + NP

```
        S
       / \
      NP   VP
            / \
           V   NP
           |
        scoffed
```

from NP → (DET) + N we can select
        NP → N

```
            S
          /   \
        NP      VP
         |      / \
         N     V   NP
         |     |
      Karen  scoffed
```

from NP → (DET) + N we can select
        NP → DET + N

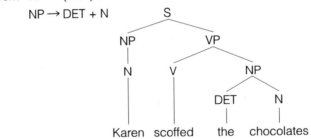

b.   S → NP + VP

```
            S
          /   \
        NP      VP
```

VP → V + NP

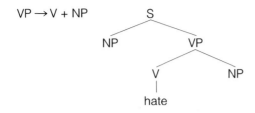

from NP → (DET) + N we can select in both cases
NP → N

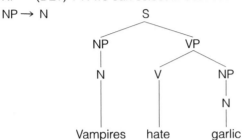

c. S → NP + VP

VP → V + NP

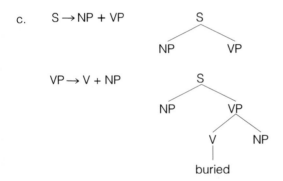

from NP → (DET) + N we can select in both cases
NP → N

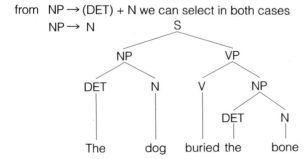

Tree diagrams for examples 1–9

1.

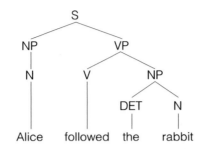

2.

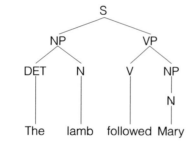

3.

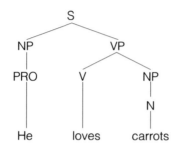

4.

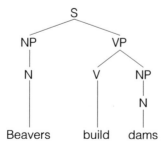

5.

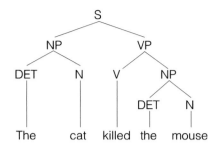

6.

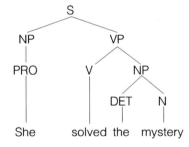

7.

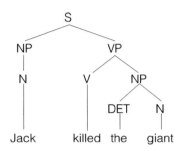

8.

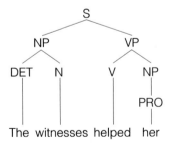

9.

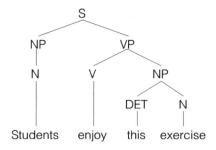

Examples on page 24:

extremely fast = AdvP → deg + Adv
seriously   = AdvP → Adv
too loudly   = AdvP → deg + Adv

Exercise 3 (page 28)

1.

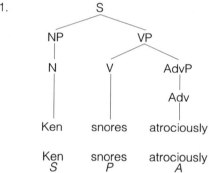

Ken   snores   atrociously
 S   P   A

2.

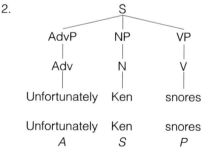

Unfortunately   Ken   snores
      A   S   P

3.

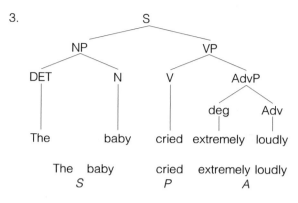

```
                        S
            NP                    VP
      DET         N         V          AdvP
                                    deg      Adv
      The        baby     cried  extremely  loudly
```

The   baby   cried   extremely loudly
      S   *P*   *A*

4.

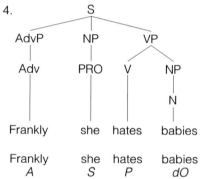

```
              S
   AdvP      NP       VP
   Adv      PRO    V      NP
                           N
  Frankly   she  hates   babies
```

Frankly   she   hates   babies
  A   *S*   *P*   *dO*

Exercise 4 (page 31)

1.

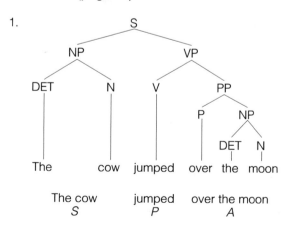

```
                  S
         NP                VP
   DET        N       V          PP
                               P      NP
                                   DET   N
   The        cow   jumped  over  the  moon
```

The cow   jumped   over the moon
  S   *P*   *A*

2.

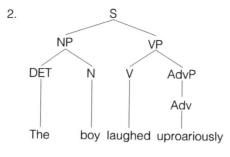

The boy   laughed   uproariously
   S   P   A

3.

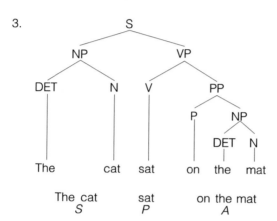

The cat   sat   on the mat
   S   P   A

4.

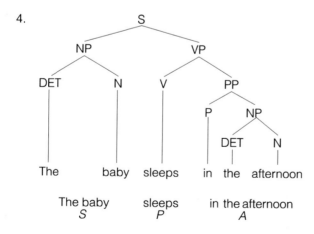

The baby   sleeps   in the afternoon
   S   P   A

5.

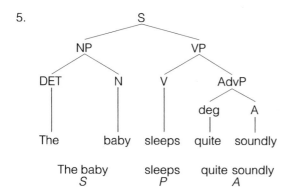

The baby   sleeps   quite soundly
S   *P*   *A*

Exercise 5   (page 38)

1.

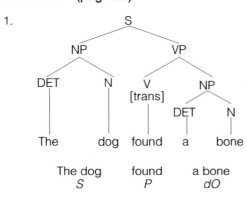

The dog   found   a bone
S   *P*   *dO*

2.

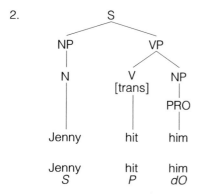

Jenny   hit   him
S   *P*   *dO*

3.

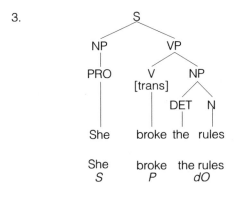

4.

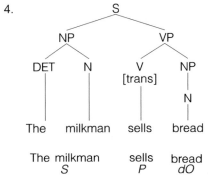

Exercise 6 (page 40)

1.

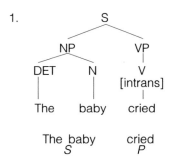

2.

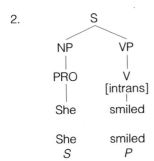

```
              S
           /     \
         NP        VP
          |         |
         PRO        V
          |      [intrans]
          |         |
         She      smiled

         She      smiled
          S         P
```

3.

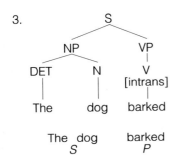

```
              S
           /     \
         NP        VP
        /   \       |
      DET    N      V
       |     |   [intrans]
       |     |      |
      The   dog   barked

      The dog    barked
          S         P
```

4.

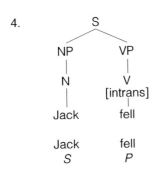

```
              S
           /     \
         NP        VP
          |         |
          N         V
          |      [intrans]
          |         |
         Jack      fell

         Jack      fell
          S         P
```

Exercise 7 (page 41)

1.

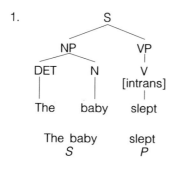

2.

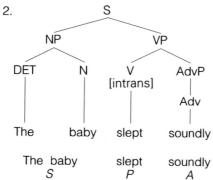

3.

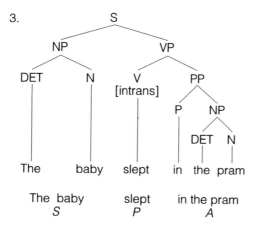

4.

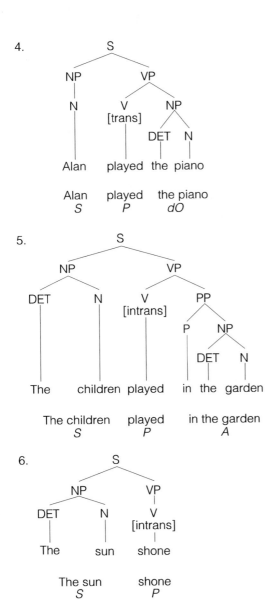

```
                    S
          ┌─────────┴─────────┐
         NP                   VP
          │              ┌─────┴─────┐
          N              V          NP
                      [trans]    ┌───┴───┐
                               DET      N
          │              │       │       │
         Alan         played   the    piano

         Alan         played   the piano
          S             P         dO
```

5.

```
                        S
            ┌───────────┴───────────┐
           NP                       VP
        ┌───┴───┐           ┌────────┴────────┐
      DET       N           V                PP
                        [intrans]        ┌────┴────┐
                                         P        NP
                                              ┌────┴────┐
                                            DET        N
        │         │           │        │     │         │
       The    children     played     in    the     garden

       The children      played        in the garden
            S               P                 A
```

6.

```
                    S
          ┌─────────┴─────────┐
         NP                   VP
      ┌───┴───┐                │
    DET       N                V
                           [intrans]
      │        │               │
     The      sun            shone

     The sun              shone
        S                   P
```

7.

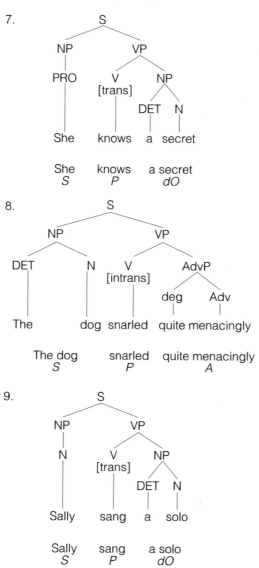

```
                    S
            ┌───────┴───────┐
           NP              VP
            │          ┌────┴────┐
           PRO         V        NP
                     [trans]   ┌──┴──┐
                              DET    N
            │          │       │     │
           She       knows     a   secret

           She       knows    a secret
            S          P         dO
```

8.

```
                         S
              ┌──────────┴──────────┐
             NP                    VP
        ┌─────┴─────┐        ┌──────┴──────┐
       DET          N        V            AdvP
                          [intrans]     ┌───┴───┐
                                       deg     Adv
        │           │          │        │       │
       The         dog      snarled   quite menacingly

      The dog              snarled    quite menacingly
         S                    P              A
```

9.

```
                    S
            ┌───────┴───────┐
           NP              VP
            │          ┌────┴────┐
            N          V        NP
                     [trans]   ┌──┴──┐
                              DET    N
            │          │       │     │
          Sally      sang      a    solo

          Sally      sang     a solo
            S          P         dO
```

10.

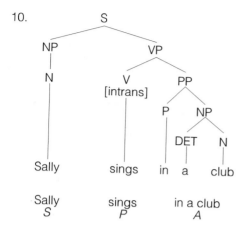

Sally sings in a club
S   P   A

The examples at 4 and 5, and 9 and 10 illustrate how some verbs can belong to more than one verb class.

Exercise 8 (page 45)

Tree diagrams

1.

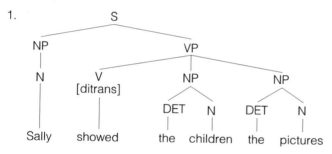

2.

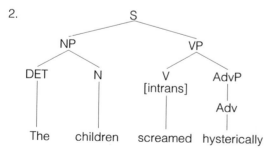

3.

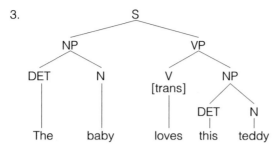

4.

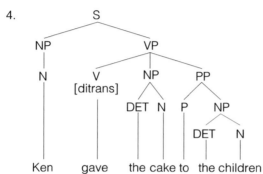

5.

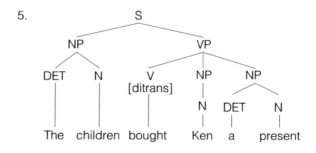

6.

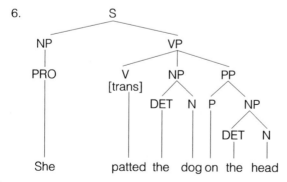

Function analysis

1. Sally   showed   the children   the pictures
       S   P   iO   dO

2. The children   screamed   hysterically
          S   P   A

3. The baby   loves   this teddy
        S   P   dO

4. Ken   gave   the cake   to the children
     S   P   dO   iO

5. The children   bought   Ken   a present
          S   P   iO   dO

6. She   patted   the dog   on the head
     S   P   dO   A

7. Ken   made   a cake   for the party
     S   P   dO   A

8. Ken   made   a cake   for Sally
     S   P   dO   iO

9. She   wrote   a letter   to the council
     S   P   dO   iO

10. She   wrote   a message   on the wall
     S   P   dO   A

Exercise 9 (page 49)

1.

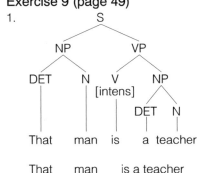

That   man   is a teacher
 S   P   sC

2.

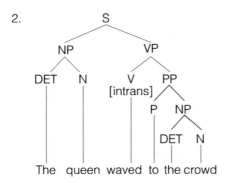

The queen   waved   to the crowd
   S   P   A

3.

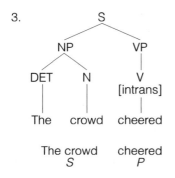

The crowd   cheered
   S   P

4.

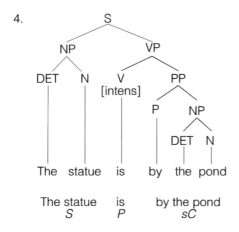

The statue   is   by the pond
   S   P   sC

5.

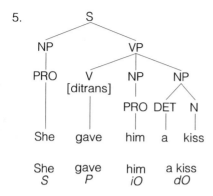

She	gave	him	a kiss
S	P	iO	dO

6.

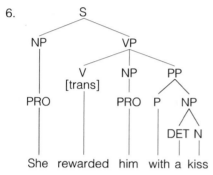

She	rewarded	him	with a kiss
S	P	dO	A

7.

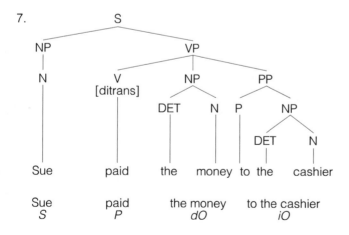

Sue	paid	the money	to the cashier
S	P	dO	iO

8.

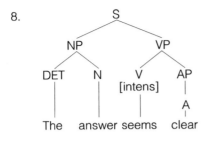

The answer   seems   clear
     S   P   sC

9.

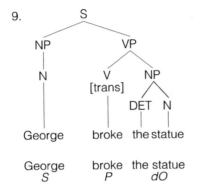

George   broke   the statue
   S   P   dO

10.

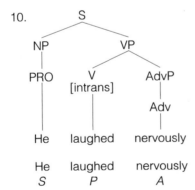

He   laughed   nervously
 S   P   A

Exercise 10 (page 50)

1.

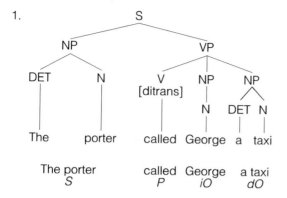

Test sentence: The porter called a taxi for George

2.

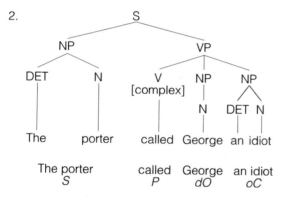

Test sentence: The porter called an idiot for George – although this may make sense in some context, the meaning has changed.

Exercise 11   (page 52)

(36a)

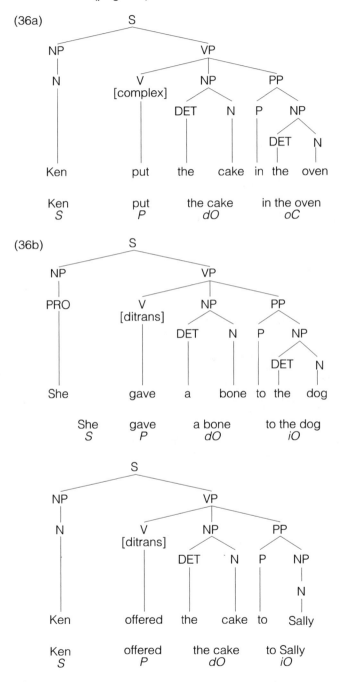

Ken	put	the cake	in the oven
S	P	dO	oC

(36b)

She	gave	a bone	to the dog
S	P	dO	iO

Ken	offered	the cake	to Sally
S	P	dO	iO

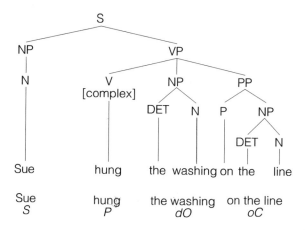

Sue hung the washing on the line

Sue	hung	the washing	on the line
S	P	dO	oC

Exercise 12 (page 55)

1.

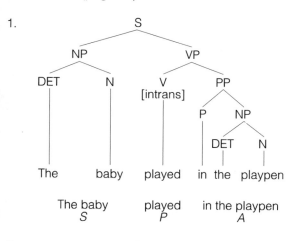

The baby played in the playpen

The baby	played	in the playpen
S	P	A

2.

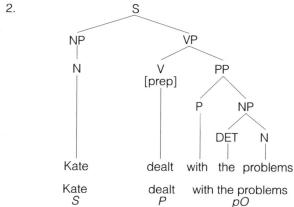

Kate dealt with the problems

Kate	dealt	with the problems
S	P	pO

3.

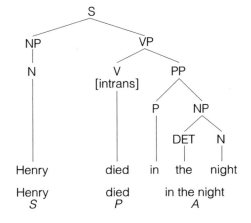

4.

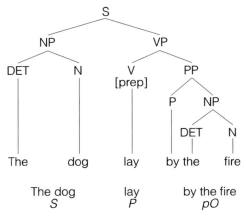

5.

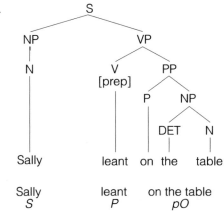

6.

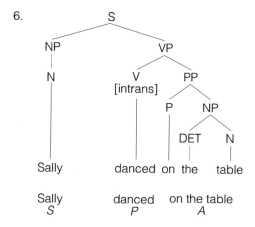

```
                    S
         ┌──────────┴──────────┐
        NP                     VP
         │              ┌──────┴──────┐
         N              V             PP
                     [intrans]   ┌────┴────┐
                                 P        NP
                                      ┌────┴────┐
                                     DET        N
                                      │         │
       Sally           danced   on   the      table

       Sally           danced     on the table
         S                P            A
```

Note: the **forms** in these examples are largely the same; the **functions** vary:

Exercise 13 (page 57)

1.

```
                    S
         ┌──────────┴──────────┐
        NP                     VP
         │              ┌──────┴──────┐
         N              V             NP
                     [trans]     ┌────┴────┐
                                DET        N
                                 │         │
      Children          hate    the      dark

      Children          hate      the dark
         S                P           dO
```

2.

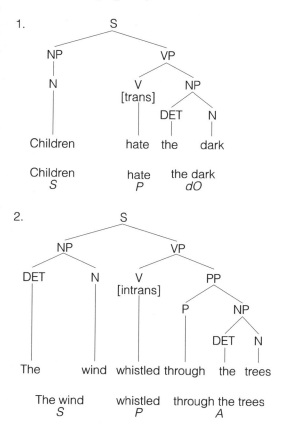

```
                         S
           ┌─────────────┴─────────────┐
          NP                           VP
       ┌───┴───┐               ┌───────┴───────┐
      DET      N               V               PP
                            [intrans]      ┌────┴────┐
                                           P        NP
                                                ┌────┴────┐
                                               DET        N
                                                │         │
      The      wind    whistled   through      the      trees

      The wind          whistled     through the trees
         S                  P               A
```

3.

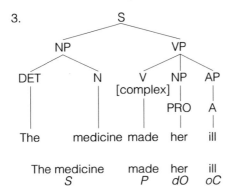

```
                        S
              ┌─────────┴─────────┐
             NP                   VP
         ┌────┴────┐      ┌───────┼───────┐
        DET        N      V       NP      AP
                       [complex]  │       │
         │         │      │      PRO      A
         │         │      │       │       │
        The     medicine made    her     ill
```

The medicine	made	her	ill
S	P	dO	oC

4.

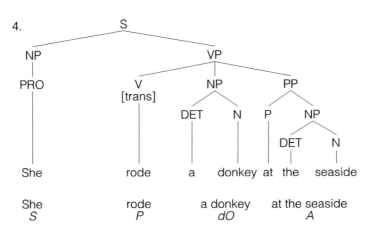

```
                          S
          ┌───────────────┴───────────────────────┐
         NP                                        VP
          │                    ┌───────────┬───────────────┐
         PRO                   V           NP              PP
                            [trans]     ┌──┴──┐         ┌───┴───┐
                                       DET    N         P       NP
                                                              ┌──┴──┐
                                                             DET    N
          │                    │        │     │       │      │     │
         She                  rode      a  donkey     at    the  seaside
```

She	rode	a donkey	at the seaside
S	P	dO	A

5.

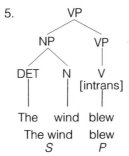

```
              VP
         ┌────┴────┐
        NP         VP
      ┌──┴──┐      │
     DET    N      V
                [intrans]
      │     │      │
     The  wind   blew
```

The wind	blew
S	P

6.

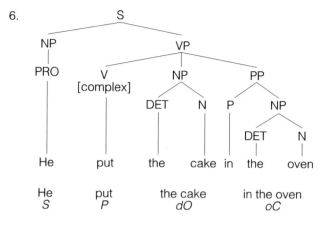

```
He        put        the cake        in the oven
S          P            dO               oC
```

7.

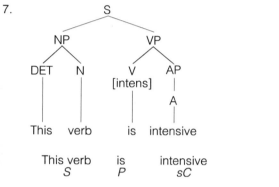

```
This verb      is        intensive
    S           P           sC
```

Imperative mood

8.

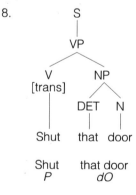

```
Shut      that door
 P           dO
```

9.

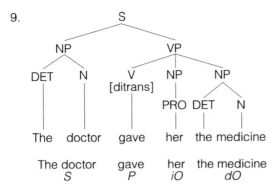

10.

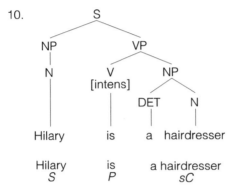

11.

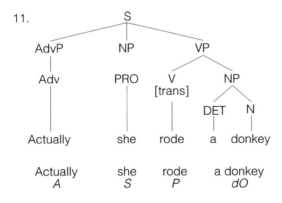

12.

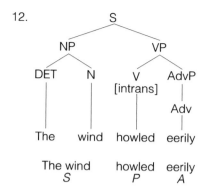

The wind   howled   eerily
     S   P   A

13.

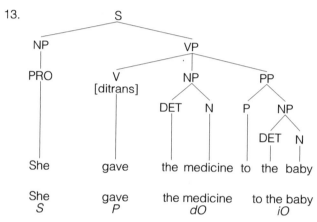

She   gave   the medicine   to the baby
  S   P   dO   iO

14.

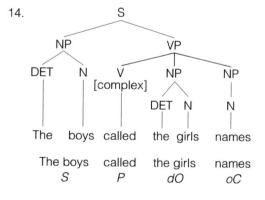

The boys   called   the girls   names
    S   P   dO   oC

15.

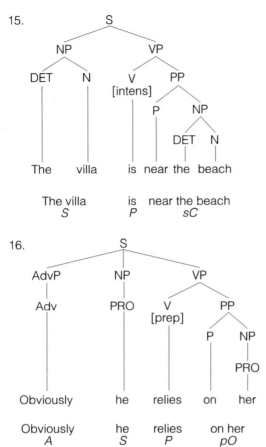

16.

Exercise 14 (page 63)

4a.

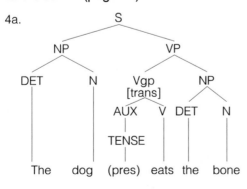

4b.

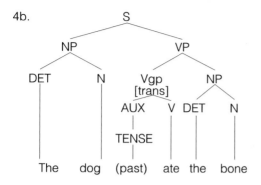

```
                        S
              ┌─────────┴─────────┐
             NP                   VP
          ┌───┴───┐          ┌────┴────┐
        DET       N        Vgp         NP
                          [trans]    ┌──┴──┐
                         ┌──┴──┐    DET    N
                        AUX    V
                         │
                       TENSE
         │        │     │     │    │     │
        The      dog  (past) ate the   bone
```

5a.

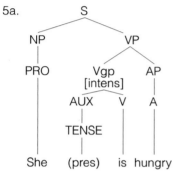

```
                  S
          ┌───────┴───────┐
         NP               VP
          │          ┌────┴────┐
        PRO        Vgp         AP
                  [intens]      │
                 ┌──┴──┐        A
                AUX    V
                 │
               TENSE
          │      │     │    │
        She   (pres)  is  hungry
```

5b.

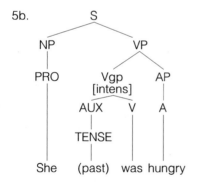

```
                  S
          ┌───────┴───────┐
         NP               VP
          │          ┌────┴────┐
        PRO        Vgp         AP
                  [intens]      │
                 ┌──┴──┐        A
                AUX    V
                 │
               TENSE
          │      │     │    │
        She   (past)  was  hungry
```

Exercise 15 (page 66)

11a.

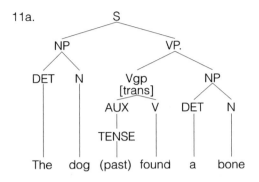

```
                        S
          NP                    VP.
      DET    N         Vgp            NP
                      [trans]
                    AUX    V    DET    N
                     |
                   TENSE
      The    dog  (past) found   a    bone
```

11b.

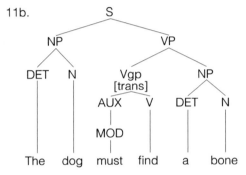

```
                        S
          NP                    VP
      DET    N         Vgp            NP
                      [trans]
                    AUX    V    DET    N
                     |
                    MOD
      The    dog   must  find    a    bone
```

11c.

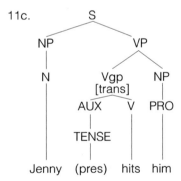

```
                  S
         NP             VP
          N      Vgp       NP
                [trans]
              AUX    V    PRO
               |
             TENSE
       Jenny (pres)  hits  him
```

11d.

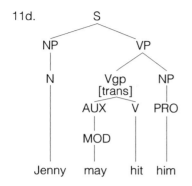

11e.

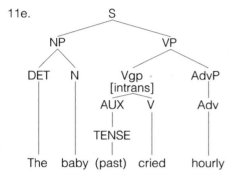

11f.

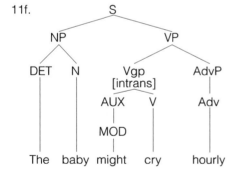

Exercise 16 (page 68)

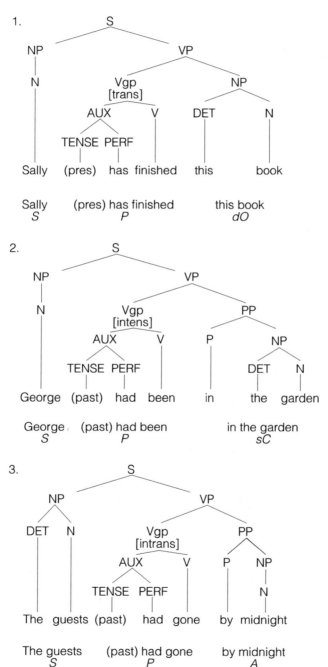

1.

Sally   (pres) has finished   this book
 S   P   dO

2.

George   (past) had been   in the garden
 S   P   sC

3.

The guests   (past) had gone   by midnight
 S   P   A

4.

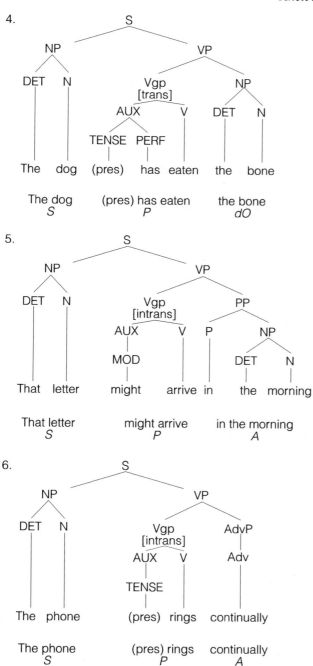

5.

6.

7.

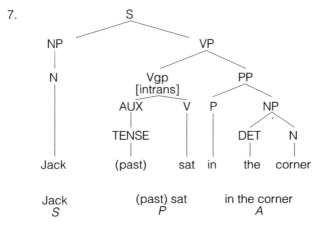

8.

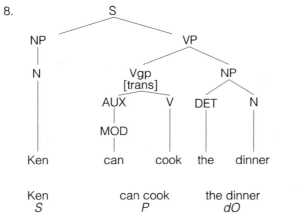

Exercise 17   (page 69)

1.

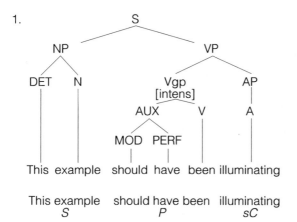

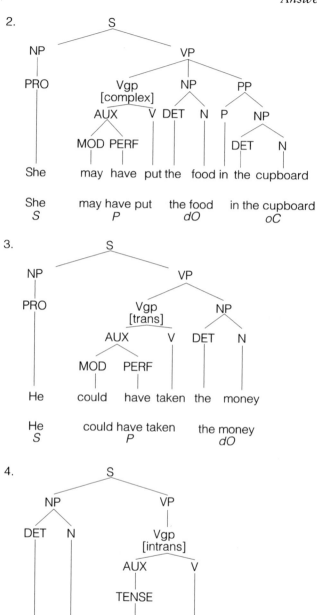

2.
```
                    S
        ┌───────────┴──────────────┐
       NP                          VP
        │              ┌───────────┼──────────┐
       PRO            Vgp          NP         PP
                   [complex]      ┌─┴─┐      ┌─┴──┐
                   ┌───┴───┐     DET  N     P   NP
                  AUX      V                   ┌──┴──┐
                ┌──┴──┐                       DET    N
               MOD  PERF
                │    │    │    │    │    │    │    │
               She  may have put the food in the cupboard
```

She	may have put	the food	in the cupboard
S	P	dO	oC

3.
```
                  S
        ┌─────────┴────────────┐
       NP                       VP
        │            ┌──────────┼──────┐
       PRO          Vgp         NP
                  [trans]      ┌─┴──┐
                ┌────┴───┐    DET   N
               AUX       V
             ┌──┴───┐
            MOD   PERF
             │      │     │     │    │
            He   could  have taken the money
```

He	could have taken	the money
S	P	dO

4.
```
                 S
        ┌────────┴────────┐
       NP                 VP
      ┌─┴─┐                │
     DET  N              Vgp
                       [intrans]
                     ┌─────┴─────┐
                    AUX          V
                     │
                   TENSE
      │     │         │          │
     The  penny     (past)    dropped
```

The penny	(past) dropped
S	P

5.

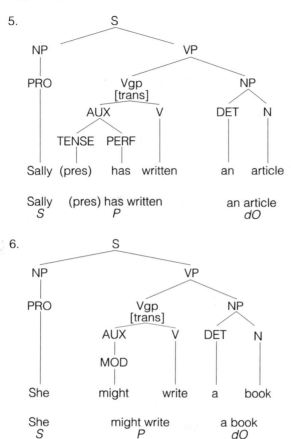

6.

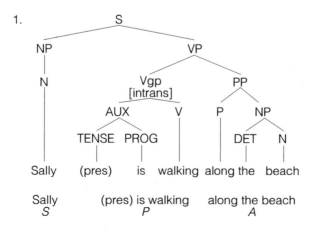

Exercise 18   (page 71)

1.

```
                      S
        ┌─────────────┴─────────────┐
       NP                           VP
        │              ┌────────────┴────────────┐
        N             Vgp                        PP
                    [intrans]              ┌──────┴──────┐
              ┌───────┴───────┐            P            NP
             AUX              V                    ┌─────┴─────┐
         ┌────┴────┐                              DET          N
       TENSE     PROG
         │         │         │            │        │          │
       Sally    (pres)      is         walking  along the   beach
```

Sally   (pres) is walking   along the beach
  S   P   A

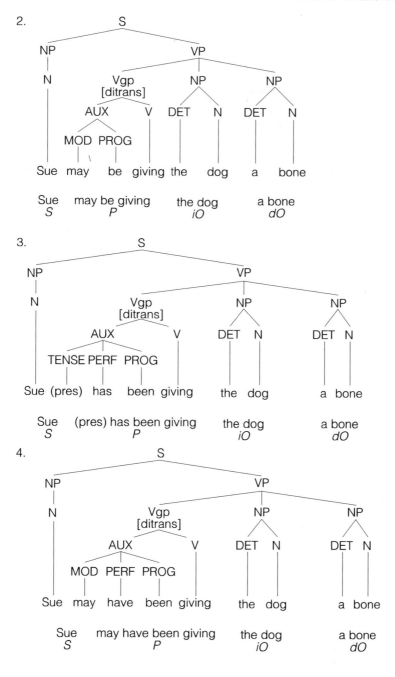

2.
```
                    S
        ┌───────────┴──────────────────┐
       NP                              VP
        │              ┌───────────┬────────────┐
        N             Vgp          NP           NP
                   [ditrans]     ┌───┴──┐     ┌───┴──┐
              ┌──────────┐ V    DET    N    DET     N
             AUX         │      │      │      │      │
           ┌──┴──┐       │      │      │      │      │
          MOD  PROG      │      │      │      │      │
           │     │       │      │      │      │      │
          Sue  may    be giving the   dog    a    bone

          Sue    may be giving     the dog      a bone
           S          P              iO           dO
```

3.
```
                    S
        ┌───────────┴──────────────────┐
       NP                              VP
        │              ┌───────────┬────────────┐
        N             Vgp          NP           NP
                   [ditrans]     ┌─┴─┐        ┌─┴─┐
              ┌──────────┐ V    DET  N       DET  N
             AUX         │      │    │        │    │
         ┌────┴────┐     │      │    │        │    │
       TENSE PERF PROG   │      │    │        │    │
         │     │    │     │      │    │        │    │
        Sue (pres) has been giving the dog    a  bone

         Sue   (pres) has been giving    the dog     a bone
          S            P                   iO          dO
```

4.
```
                    S
        ┌───────────┴──────────────────┐
       NP                              VP
        │              ┌───────────┬────────────┐
        N             Vgp          NP           NP
                   [ditrans]     ┌─┴─┐        ┌─┴─┐
              ┌──────────┐ V    DET  N       DET  N
             AUX         │      │    │        │    │
         ┌────┴────┐     │      │    │        │    │
        MOD PERF PROG    │      │    │        │    │
         │    │    │      │      │    │        │    │
        Sue  may have been giving the dog     a  bone

         Sue    may have been giving    the dog      a bone
          S            P                  iO           dO
```

5.   This sentence is ambiguous and has more than one interpretation:

5a.

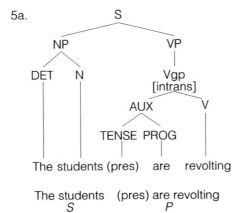

The students   (pres) are revolting
      S   P

Meaning: the students are in the throes of revolution

5b.

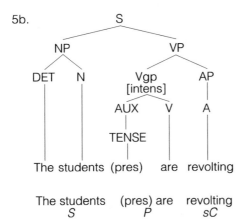

The students   (pres) are   revolting
      S   P   sC

Meaning: the speaker/writer has a low opinion of student qualities

6. (She) must have run
7. (She) had been running
8. (She) must be running
9. (She) is running
10. (She) must have been running
11. (She) ran
12. (She) has run

Exercise 19 (page 75)

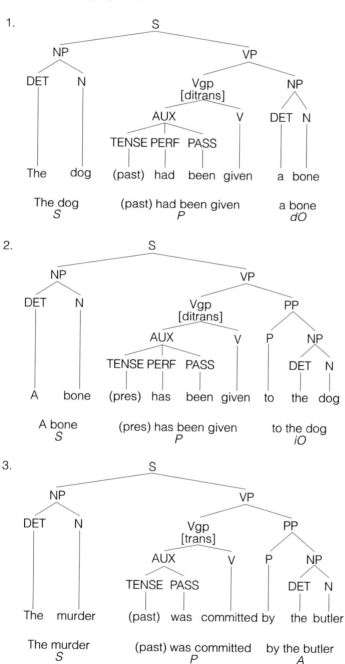

1.
The dog   (past) had been given   a bone
S   P   dO

2.
A bone   (pres) has been given   to the dog
S   P   iO

3.
The murder   (past) was committed   by the butler
S   P   A

4.

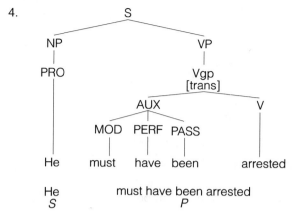

He   must have been arrested
S   P

5.

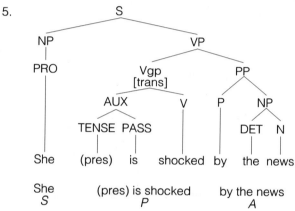

She   (pres) is shocked   by the news
S   P   A

6. (She) must have been seen

7. (She) must have seen

8. (She) was being seen

9. (She) has seen

10. (She) saw

Exercise 20 (page 77)

1.

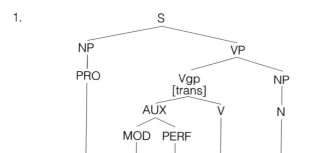

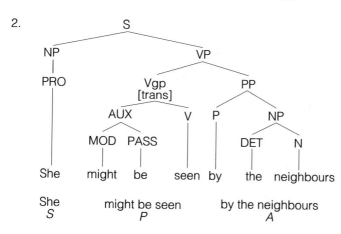

He
S   may have said   something
                 P   dO

2.

She
S   might be seen   by the neighbours
               P   A

3.

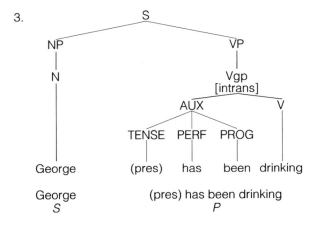

```
                    S
          /                    \
        NP                      VP
         |                       |
         N                      Vgp
                              [intrans]
                             /         \
                          AUX           V
                        /   |   \
                    TENSE  PERF  PROG
                      |     |     |       |
    George         (pres)  has   been  drinking

    George              (pres) has been drinking
      S                            P
```

4.

```
                         S
            /                         \
          NP                           VP
           |                       /         \
           N                    VgP           AdvP
                              [intrans]         |
                             /        \        Adv
                          AUX          V
                           |
                         TENSE
                           |          |       |      |
   George     (pres)     does       drink  heavily

   George              (pres) does drink    heavily
     S                         P                A
```

5.

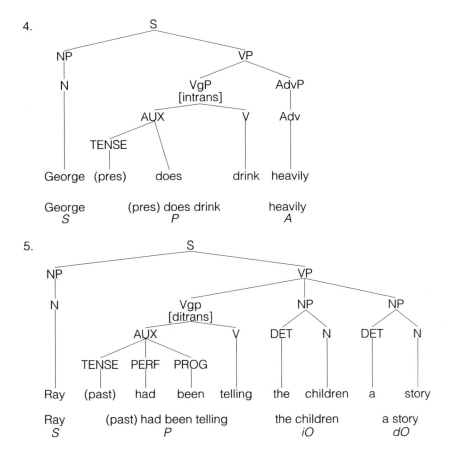

```
                              S
         /                                         \
       NP                                           VP
        |                          /                 |            \
        N                        Vgp                 NP            NP
                              [ditrans]             /   \         /   \
                             /        \           DET    N      DET    N
                          AUX          V
                        /   |   \
                    TENSE  PERF  PROG
        |            |      |     |       |      |      |        |      |
       Ray        (past)   had   been  telling  the  children   a    story

       Ray              (past) had been telling     the children    a story
        S                         P                      iO            dO
```

6.

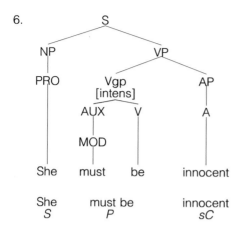

7.

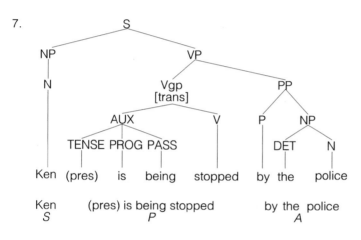

8.

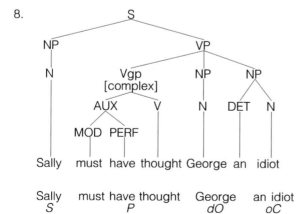

9.

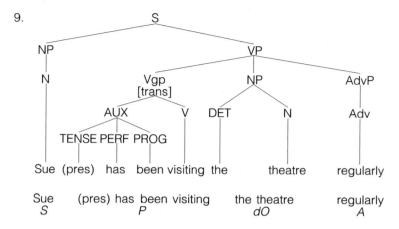

Sue	(pres) has been visiting	the theatre	regularly
S	*P*	*dO*	*A*

10.

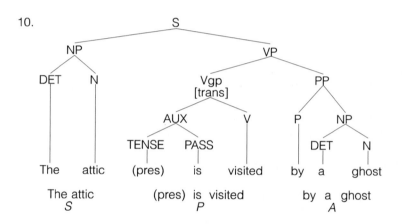

The attic	(pres) is visited	by a ghost
S	*P*	*A*

11.

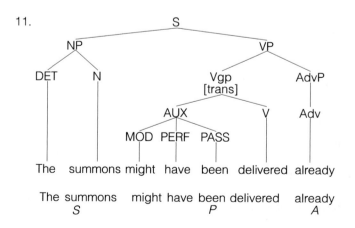

The summons	might have been delivered	already
S	*P*	*A*

Exercise 21 (page 89)

1.

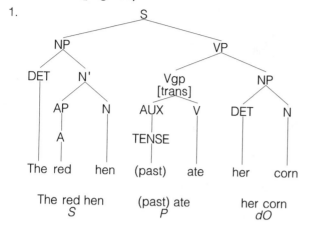

2.

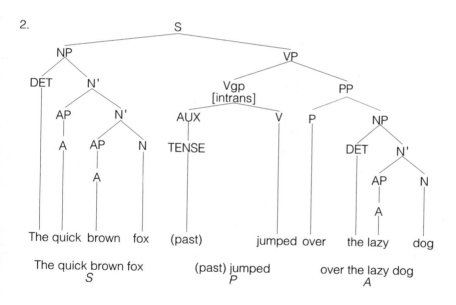

3.

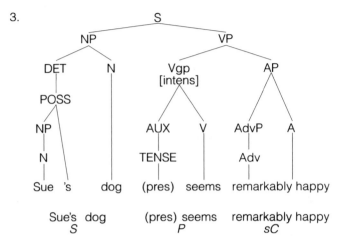

4.

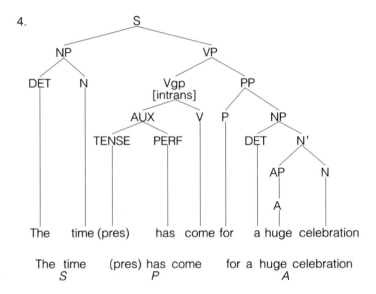

5.

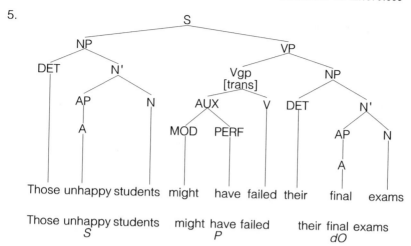

6.

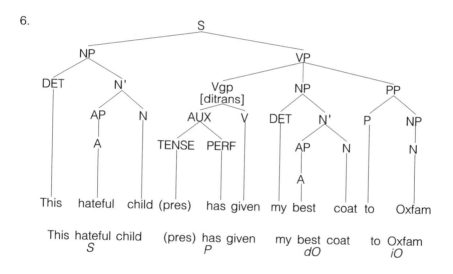

Exercise 22 (page 91)

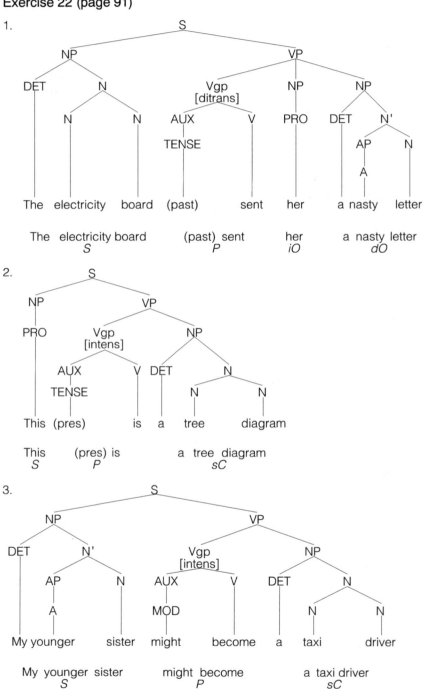

1.

The electricity board (past) sent her a nasty letter

The electricity board   (past) sent   her   a nasty letter
            S   P   iO   dO

2.

This (pres) is a tree diagram

This   (pres) is   a tree diagram
  S   P   sC

3.

My younger sister might become a taxi driver

My younger sister   might become   a taxi driver
       S   P   sC

Exercise 23 (page 95)

1.

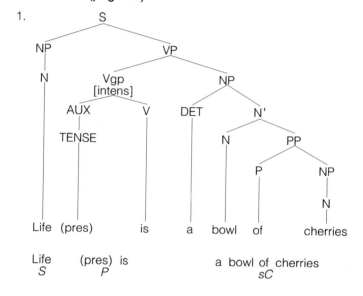

2.

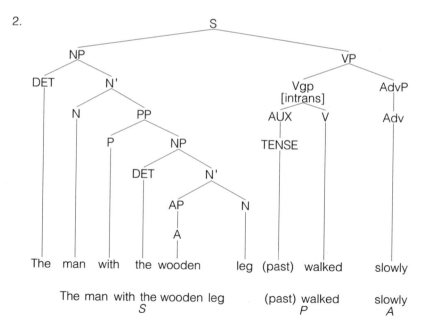

3.

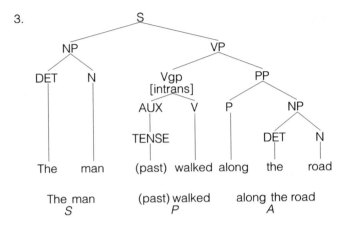

The man   (past) walked   along the road
  S   P   A

4. This sentence is ambiguous and has more than one interpretation:

4a.

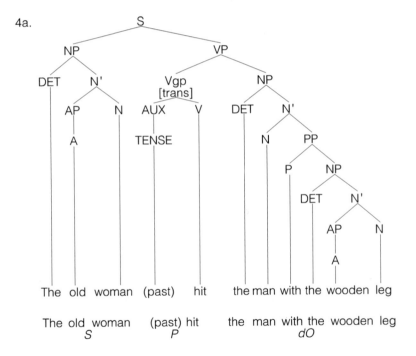

The old woman   (past) hit   the man with the wooden leg
      S   P   dO

Meaning: the man who had a wooden leg was hit by the woman by object unknown.

4b.

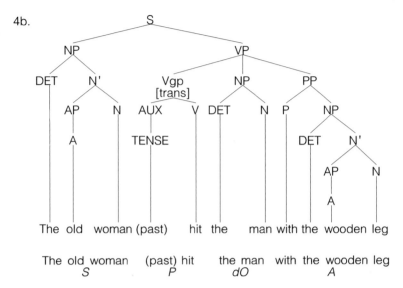

The old woman (past) hit the man with the wooden leg

The old woman (past) hit the man with the wooden leg
S   P   dO   A

Meaning: the old woman used a wooden leg to hit the man with.

5.

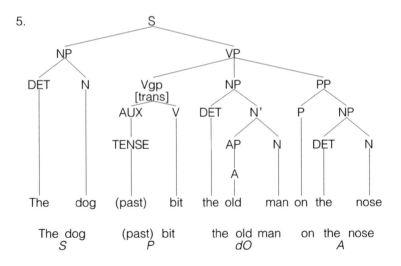

The dog (past) bit the old man on the nose

The dog (past) bit the old man on the nose
S   P   dO   A

6.

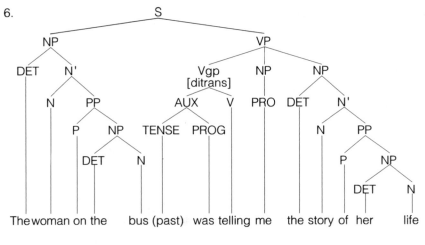

The woman on the bus	(past) was telling	me	the story of her life
S	P	iO	dO

Exercise 24 (page 98)

1.

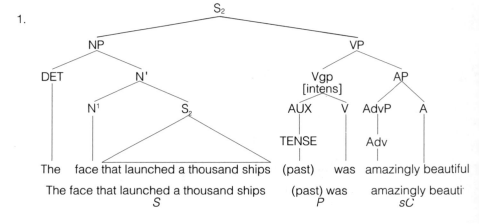

The face that launched a thousand ships	(past) was	amazingly beauti·
S	P	sC

2.

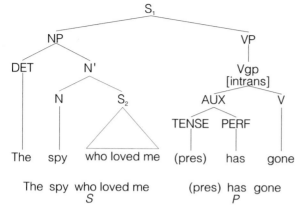

The spy who loved me   (pres) has gone
         S   P

3.

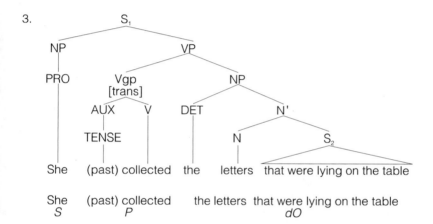

She   (past) collected   the letters that were lying on the table
 S   P   dO

4.

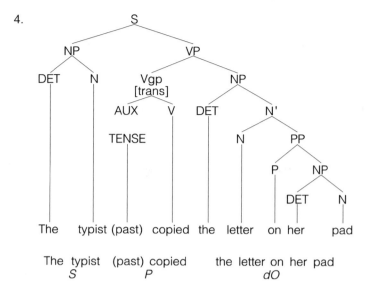

5.

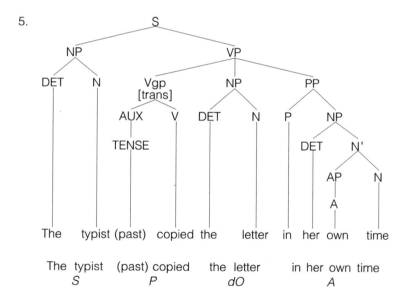

6. This sentence is ambiguous and has more than one interpretation:

6a.

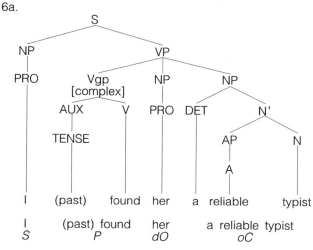

Meaning: I found her to be a reliable typist

6b.

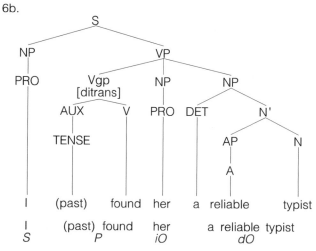

Meaning: I found a reliable typist for her.

Compare this with the example at 7 below.

7.

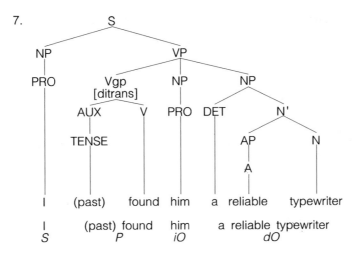

8.

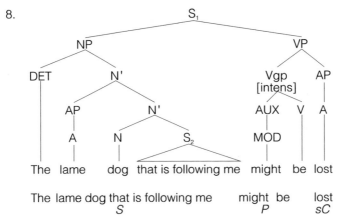

Exercise 25 (page 104)

1.

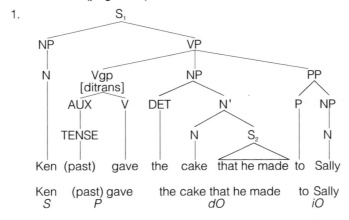

2.

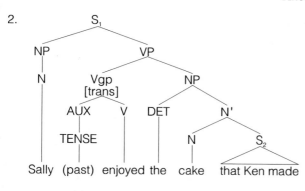

```
                    S₁
         NP                  VP
          N          Vgp            NP
                    [trans]
               AUX      V     DET        N'
                                      N      S₂
              TENSE
        Sally (past) enjoyed  the   cake   that Ken made
```

Sally (past) enjoyed   the cake that Ken made
 S   P   dO

3.

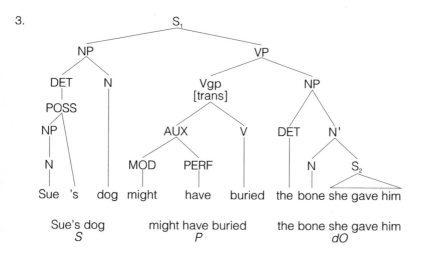

```
                              S₁
          NP                              VP
     DET       N              Vgp               NP
                             [trans]
    POSS                 AUX        V       DET      N'
    NP                                            N      S₂
     N                MOD    PERF
    Sue  's   dog   might   have   buried  the bone she gave him
```

Sue's dog   might have buried   the bone she gave him
   S   P   dO

4.

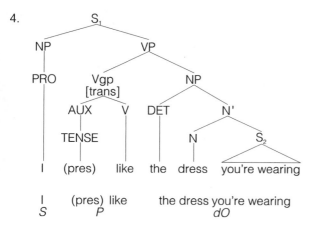

```
           S₁
   NP            VP
  PRO     Vgp          NP
         [trans]
      AUX     V    DET       N'
                          N      S₂
     TENSE
   I   (pres) like  the  dress  you're wearing
```

 I   (pres) like   the dress you're wearing
 S   P   dO

5.

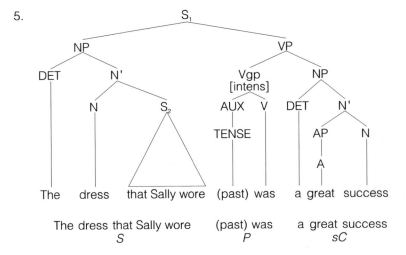

The dress that Sally wore	(past) was	a great success
S	P	sC

Exercise 26 (page 105)

1.

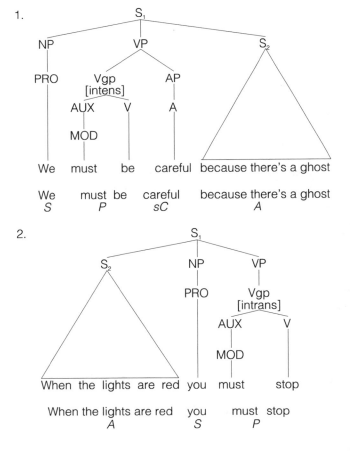

We	must be	careful	because there's a ghost
S	P	sC	A

2.

When the lights are red	you	must stop
A	S	P

3.

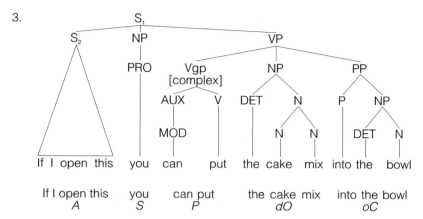

If I open this | you | can put | the cake mix | into the bowl
A | S | P | dO | oC

Exercise 27 (page 109)

1. Adverbial Clause

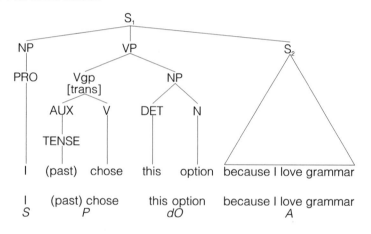

I | (past) chose | this option | because I love grammar
S | P | dO | A

2. Noun Clause

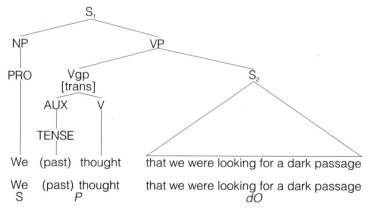

We | (past) thought | that we were looking for a dark passage
S | P | dO

3. Relative Clause

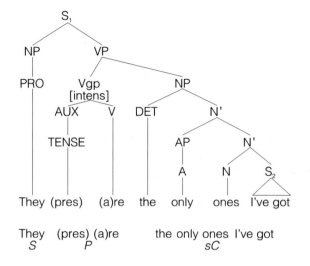

They   (pres) (a)re   the only ones I've got
  S   P   sC

4. Noun Clause

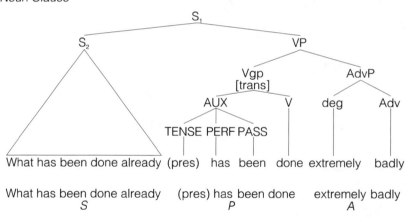

What has been done already   (pres) has been done   extremely badly
          S   P   A

5. *Noun Clause*

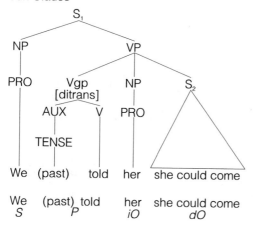

We (past) told her she could come
S   P   iO   dO

6. *Adverbial Clause*

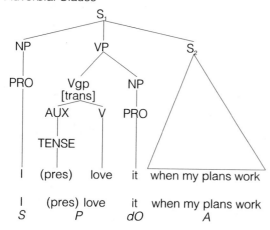

I (pres) love it when my plans work
S   P   dO   A

7. Noun Clause

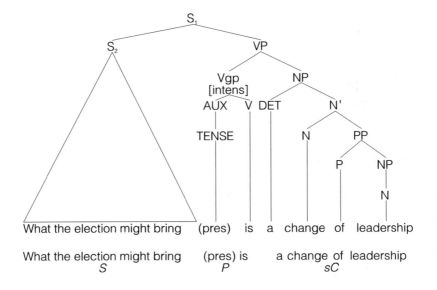

Exercise 28 (page 111)

1. Complement Clause: complement of A

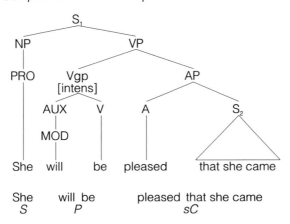

2. *Noun Clause*

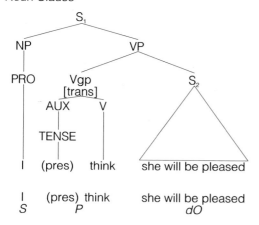

	(pres) think	she will be pleased
S	P	dO

3. *Complement Clause: subject complement*

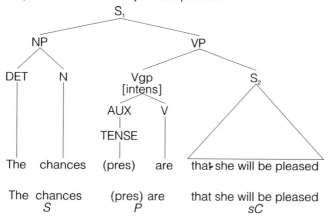

The chances	(pres) are	that she will be pleased
S	P	sC

Exercise 29 (page 115)

1.

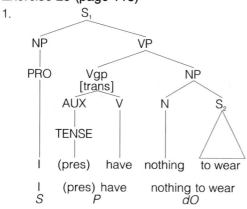

	(pres) have	nothing to wear
S	P	dO

2.

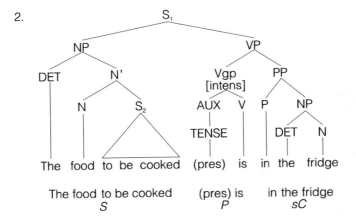

The food to be cooked   (pres) is   in the fridge
            S   P   sC

3.

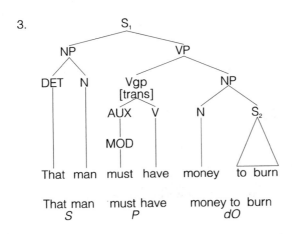

That man   must have   money to burn
     S   P   dO

4.

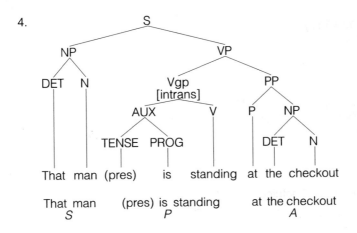

That man   (pres) is standing   at the checkout
     S   P   A

5.

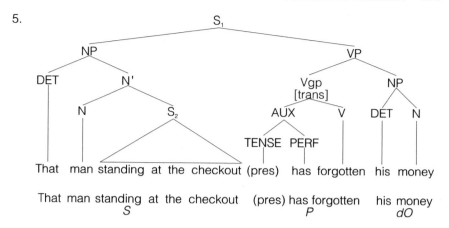

That man standing at the checkout (pres) has forgotten his money
              S   P   dO

6.

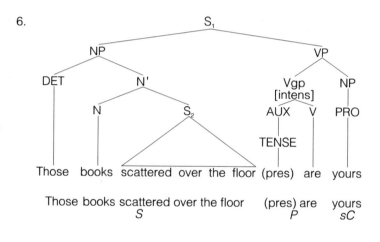

Those books scattered over the floor (pres) are yours
              S   P   sC

7.

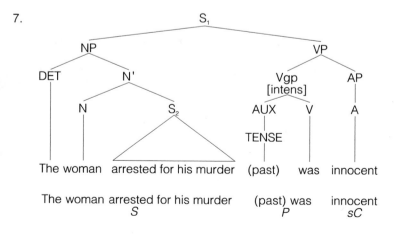

The woman arrested for his murder (past) was innocent
               S   P   sC

8.

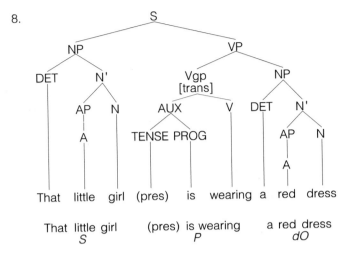

That little girl   (pres) is wearing   a red dress
      S   P   dO

9.

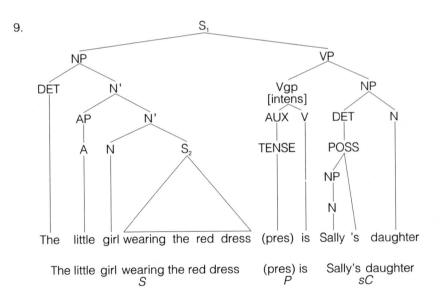

The little girl wearing the red dress   (pres) is   Sally's daughter
                  S   P   sC

Exercise 30 (page 117)

1.

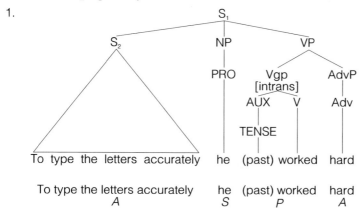

To type the letters accurately	he	(past) worked	hard
A	*S*	*P*	*A*

2.

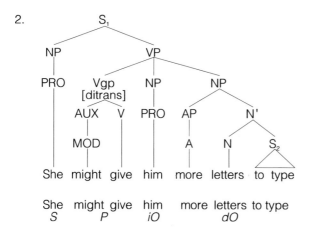

She	might give	him	more letters to type
S	*P*	*iO*	*dO*

3.

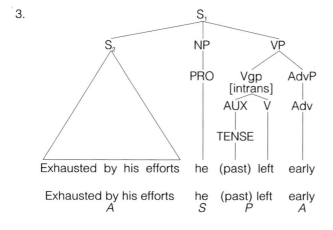

Exhausted by his efforts	he	(past) left	early
A	*S*	*P*	*A*

4.

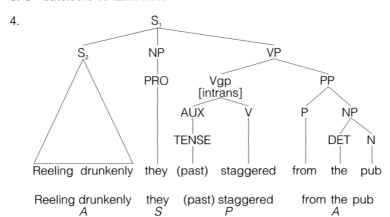

Reeling drunkenly   they   (past) staggered   from the pub
        A   S   P   A

5.

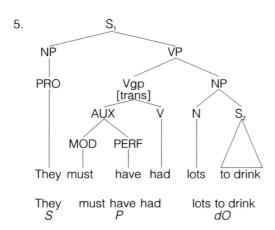

They   must have had   lots to drink
  S   P   dO

Exercise 31 (page 119)

1.

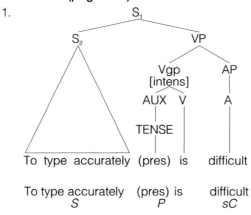

To type accurately   (pres) is   difficult
         S   P   sC

2.

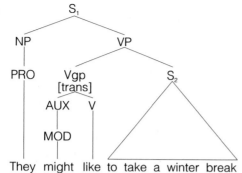

They might like to take a winter break

They   might like   to take a winter break
  S   P   dO

3.

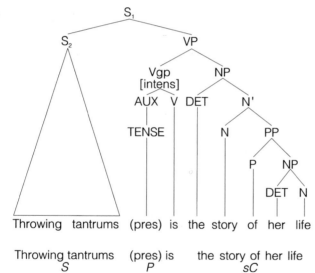

Throwing tantrums (pres) is the story of her life

Throwing tantrums   (pres) is   the story of her life
      S   P   sC

4.

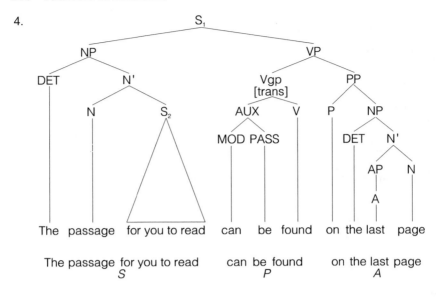

The passage for you to read | can be found | on the last page
S   P   A

5.

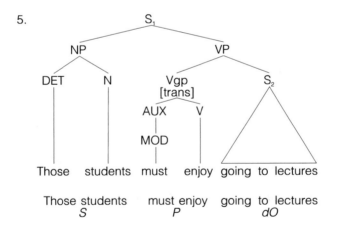

Those students | must enjoy | going to lectures
S   P   dO

6.

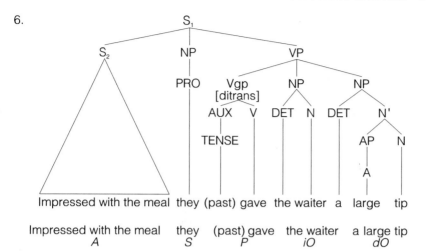

Impressed with the meal they (past) gave the waiter a large tip

Impressed with the meal	they	(past) gave	the waiter	a large tip
A	S	P	iO	dO

Exercise 32 (page 123)

1.

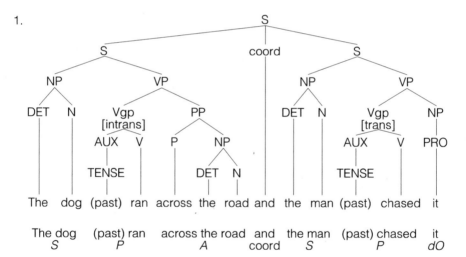

The dog (past) ran across the road and the man (past) chased it

The dog	(past) ran	across the road	and	the man	(past) chased	it
S	P	A	coord	S	P	dO

2.

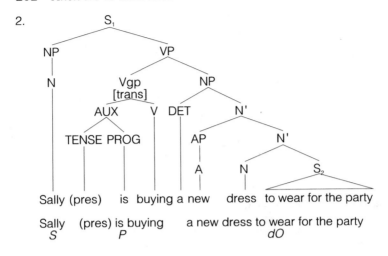

3.

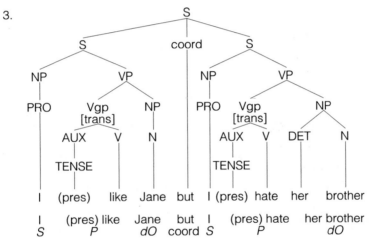

4.

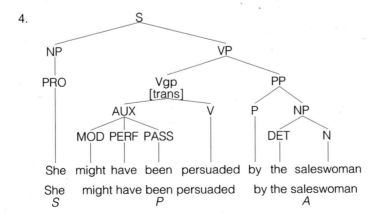

5.

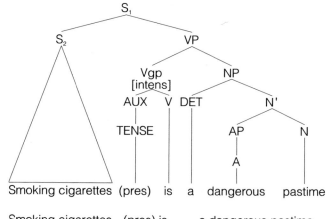

Smoking cigarettes (pres) is a dangerous pastime

Smoking cigarettes	(pres) is	a dangerous pastime
S	P	sC

6.

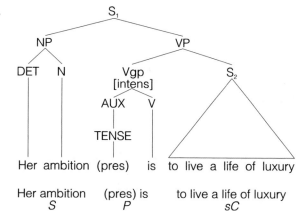

Her ambition (pres) is to live a life of luxury

Her ambition	(pres) is	to live a life of luxury
S	P	sC

7. *Imperative mood*

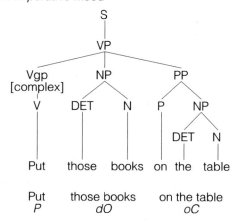

Put those books on the table

Put	those books	on the table
P	dO	oC

8.

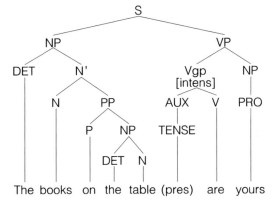

9.

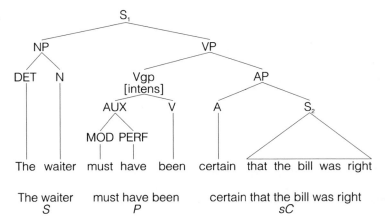

10.

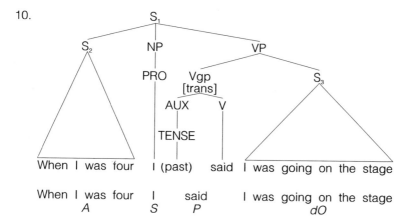

	When I was four	I	said	I was going on the stage
	A	S	P	dO

Main clause: *I said*
Subordinate adverbial clause: *When I was four*
Subordinate noun clause: *I was going on the stage*

Further Reading

I recommend the following texts as the next step in your studies.

For syntax study:

Burton-Roberts, Noel (1986) *Analysing Sentences*, Longman.
Huddleston, Rodney (1988) *English Grammar: an outline*, Cambridge University Press.

As an introduction to transformational grammar, working at a more complex level, but readable:

Radford, Andrew (1988) *Transformational Grammar: a first course*, Cambridge University Press.

For the description of English grammar:

Leech, Geoffrey, Margaret Deuchar and Robert Hoogenraad (1982) *English Grammar for Today*.
Quirk, Randolph and Sidney Greenbaum (1973) *A University Grammar of English*, Longman.

You may need to check the use of terminology in any follow up text. For instance, the expression 'Verb Phrase' can be used to describe the predicate, as in this book, or to describe what I have labelled the 'Verb Group'. Make sure you are aware of what each writer means by their use of terminology as you proceed.

Index